A Gift From God

Gregory & Patricia Kelly

AmErica House
Baltimore

First printing

ISBN: 1-59129-126-7
PUBLISHED BY AMERICA HOUSE BOOK
PUBLISHERS
www.publishamerica.com
Baltimore

Printed in the United States of America

We would like to dedicate this book to
the memory of my mother,
Leola and to
Our precious daughter,
Kimberly

Acknowledgments

The many people that we are indebted are too numerous to name individually, but there are certain individuals that we would like to recognize. First, we are grateful to our father and mother, Reginald and Thelma Dunn, who have encouraged us every step of the way. Our dear brother Michael Dunn and cousin Sharon Lewis, who has helped us to persevere throughout writing this book. And to our dear friend Johanna Giraud, who has been there always.

PREFACE

When you were a little girl, as faraway as you can remember, what was one of your biggest dreams? From the beginning, while you were still in the crib, one of the toys that were presented to you was your very first doll. That doll you treasured! You slept with that doll, you ate with that doll, and you took that doll every place you went. That doll became a part of your family. As time went on, you would be given more dolls of different collections, and those too you would add to the family that you fabricated, originating with your very first doll.

As you got older, you would receive other toys, such as a baby carriage, bottles for your doll, a kitchen set, ironing board and iron, and other necessary things that seemed to be nurturing you into becoming a wife and mother.

As the years passed by and you entered your adolescence, your maternal instincts changed from dolls to baby-sitting for other couples children. After your babysitting you would leave and go home, and once you would reach your destination you'd prepare for bed because it would be late and then you would lie awake in your bed and fantasize of your Prince Charming, who in the future would whisk you off your feet and you would marry and you both would have children. You would even select the names of your children and you would decide how many boys and how many girls you would have. You had it all outlined.

Now adulthood has entered. You found your Prince Charming and you got married, and had your dream wedding. You are so blissful together. Time would pass and both of you would decide to start that family you always dreamed about.

The calendar moved on to months, then years, and even decades and the apprehension of getting older started progressively approaching. There was no pregnancy! Fear set in — then despair — then disaster. Your biggest dream seemed to have turned into a nightmare. Or did it? Everything you thought and all your maternal feelings have come to a halt, because so far, you have not had that wonderful gift from God!

CHAPTER ONE
Once upon a Time

It was a hot summer day in July and the year was 1969. She was seated at her desk of her place of employment, she worked in the career of a secretary for a record company. She had only been out of high school for two years and she was delighting in her independence. She was now a full time wage earner and collecting a weekly paycheck.

She reminisces sitting at her desk at work and at that moment she glanced up and detected this young man walk into her office. She recalls saying hello and he answered the same. She paid him no notice, nevertheless does recall that she had never seen him before. She was slightly curious to find out who he was and questioned one of her co-workers. Someone confirmed that he was a new employee of the company. As the days went ahead, she and the new employee became friends. They enjoyed being together and each respected their friendship. He appeared to be a remarkably nice person, with an inspiring future. He was also going to college at night, as was she. He seemed to be a good catch for someone. At this time he had a girlfriend and she a boyfriend, so anything other than a friendship had not entered their mind.

As their friendship started to improve they would share secrets with each other, they went to lunch together, they laughed together, and they were there for each other, but still nothing beyond friendship ever entered their minds. He was from Brooklyn and she was from Queens. The distance seemed so faraway, as if they were from two different planets. But it was a friendship that grew each day and they were becoming inseparable, when you saw one you saw the other.

A year and a half have now passed...to the month of December and the year was 1970. An employee at work was having a party and both were invited and so they agreed to go together since he had access to a car. They were positively enjoying themselves. This was the first time, which the duo went out together in a party atmosphere. She caught herself keeping an eye on him as he danced and she noticed how he was dressed up and how exceptional he looked. He, also, was looking at her differently. It seemed like the chemistry between the two of them started growing into a little more than just a friendship as the night moved on. This was the year and the month that the two planets would come together and create a sonic BOOM... of love. This was bound to be the day that the two would start to have their lives recreated.

They started dating and began to notice different qualities in each other that they were not able to recognize as friends. It is really a positive when two people who begin a relationship being friends can have a relationship that blossoms into a boyfriend and girlfriend. The reason I think so is because as friends you are not trying to make an impression with each other and you can be yourself. You learn each other's good and bad capabilities. I feel these two were blessed to be able to have a genuine friendship for a year and a half and can now be able to go on a discovery that is contrary to their previous existence... as a couple.

They were both born in April and in the year 1950; he was only nine days older than she was. He was from a large family with three brothers and four sisters, and she was from a small family with just one brother. They realized that they both had the same dreams, with similar likes and dislikes. As the days and months sped by, they became closer with each passing day. They were growing to be inseparable. They worked together on the same job, they ate together at lunch, they enjoyed each other's companionship after work, and they did everything together. Things started to generate into a more serious relationship.

They began daydreaming of the day that the two would get married and have a family. Since he was from a large family and she a small family, they decided to pick a middle number and have four children. They discussed the kind of house they would purchase, you know the type, the typical dream house, and the beautiful small house with the white picket fence and let's not forget the dog. They had such wonderful dreams; ones that they just knew would not disappoint them and that one-day it would all come to pass.

He was still going to college at night; however, he was not satisfied with his choices, so he decided to change his direction and switch to a trade school and become an electrician. He really enjoyed working with his hands; he truly had an ability to repair almost anything. He went to school at night and he was an electrical apprentice in the day. He was on his way in acquiring a remarkably successful future. With all seeming to be falling into place, she was working for a good company and making good money also, his future was under way. So they both decided that it was time to set a date for their wedding, and that period of time became January 22, 1972. They were so blissful and ecstatic, they could not wait to plan for the biggest day of their lives and that day would be their wedding day. This day would be the opening of an extraordinary future for the both of them... together.

So now the story begins with the life and story of Cinderella and her Prince Charming...

This was the first time that she did not need an alarm clock to awaken her this exceptional morning. This was it, her **BIG DAY**. The day that she waited months for. The day that she seemed to have prepared for her whole life... **HER**

WONDERFUL WEDDING DAY! It was a beautiful winter morning, the sun was shining, the birds were singing, and it wasn't excessively cold. This was the day, January 22, 1972, the day that her Cinderella fantasy was about to commence.

She leaped right up out of the bed to prepare for the happiest day of her life. She was too excited to eat anything. The only thing on her mind was the big day of dream-filled events. She somewhat wished that this day could stand still. She wanted to keep every moment of the day fixed in her mind so that it would last forever.

Everything seemed to go so smoothly. She had all her bridesmaids with her. They were all giggling and talking, sounding like little mice, while they were preparing for the day. She never realized how much excitement it was to get dressed. All of them were running back and forth, getting into each other's way but still they were able to get the job accomplished. The bridesmaids even had time to assist the bride as she prepared for her day. Her mother just stood back with the biggest smile and with tears in her eyes as she watched her little girl who seemed to grow up so fast, about to become someone's wife.

The entire process involved numerous hours. Everything had to be flawless. Her hair, her makeup, her gown and veil, it all had to be perfect. At last, the final results! She got to see herself, for the first time, fully dressed in a full-length mirror. She, indeed, went from a girl, who just hours ago got out of bed with her pajamas on, and into a woman, who truly looked like a Princess, all dressed up in her beautiful wedding gown. She was so happy and it felt like every emotion a woman could experience she was feeling and all was about to explode, but she knew that she had to hold her emotions under restraint as to not smear her makeup. This was it! They were all, at last, prepared to leave for the church and all proceeded downstairs to their chariots. The limousines were all lined up in a single file, to take the bride, her bridesmaids, and her parents to the church. The fantasy was now becoming a reality. Her long anticipated dreams were about to come true.

The ride in the limousines truly made you feel like royalty. The horns from the cars blared "here comes the bride." People watched and some waved, it was so much fun for them all. Before they knew it, they were all in front of the church. As they entered the rear of the church, they could hear the whispers of about 200 guests seated in the pew. All were looking forward to this special day.

She and her bridesmaids stood in the back of the church as they waited for the motion to let them know when the procedure would start. They were so excited and a little nervous. There long-anticipated moment was finally here... the music began and they all gave each other one final glance, and the first bridesmaid proceeded down the aisle. She watched them one by one take their leave and she knew her time was drawing near. As the flower girl prepared her exit, she held her father's arm and they both prepared to make that journey down that long walkway. All the guests stood up as she and her father marched slowly down the aisle. All eyes were upon her. She truly felt like a Cinderella and there stood her Prince Charming waiting for his Princess' arrival.

The soon to be husband and wife came together and joined hands and the minister started the words of the marriage vows. They were both so nervous. The words kept echoing in their ears — "for richer or poorer, for better or worse, in sickness and in health, and until death do you part." They both never realized how meaningful those words were. And now the ultimate words were sounded, "you are now husband and wife, you may kiss your bride." They exchanged their first kiss as husband and wife and all applauded. They turned and faced their family and friends with a tremendous smile and proceeded back down the aisle walking hand in hand to receive their congratulations and to leave for the big gala to celebrate the happy event at the reception hall with their many guests.

This was instituting the commencement of the remainder of their lives.

It was thrilling for them, moving into their very own apartment. This was their castle. This was the first time that both have left their parent's home. They couldn't wait until they would start decorating and begin adding their own distinctive style. They moved in with a limited amount of furniture, with just the essentials. Now it was time to start filling up the rooms and so they set out to go furniture shopping. They were relieved when they realized that both had the same preference in furniture, so that made it easier, since they were in agreement with their selections. As time moved on, they had chosen a beautiful living room and dining room set. It was so awesome in believing that this was all theirs, furniture and all.

Also, on the schedule was that they had to go grocery shopping. That was really fun because they could buy all the things they liked and not all the things they were forced to eat while growing up. They tried everything that new couples do to make their apartment a home. Her biggest venture was trying to acquire some cooking ability because she had none. He became her victim of many experimental meals, some he barely escaped. Sometimes they had expectation that they would have to call the fire department for burning food, it was positively a time and chance case, and with lots of love on his part, he was able to have courage to swallow the food. I'm confident they both lost some pounds during those early months, but he was patient and she was very persistent until finally meals took a turn for the better.

It was an entirely new life. All her toys that she had as a child, her kitchen set, her ironing board and iron, all became a part of her adult world. And then... Oh no! It appeared as though the honeymoon was over! Their preparation for adulthood was now being tested. Wait a minute, they HAD to go to work and be responsible for themselves, they HAD to be the ones to pay the rent and all the other bills, and they HAD to buy food in order to live. They at no time realized all the had to's.

Then they started questioning where is her Prince Charming and where is his Cinderella? They thought that they both got along so well before they lived together. They now discovered that both had different ways of accomplishing things and each one wanted to be correct, and how can both be correct and continue to live in accord. They had to discover how to find a middle ground. They recognized that they both had some growing up to achieve. The words of the marriage vows kept echoing in their ears, "for better or worse." They knew that they had to reacquaint themselves to each other all over again, but this time as husband and wife. It was exciting as they sailed through their new discoveries as husband and wife, and as long as they encountered their findings... together. You see, marriage is 100% by both partners and not just one and these two were determined that they were going to develop into a partnership, as husband and wife, however not in name only but also be recognized as a happily married couple in the process. They both knew that they were now a component of the adult married world!

They matured together as a young married couple. They learned how to forgive each other's weaknesses, because we all have them. They also learned to encourage each other and most importantly they learned how to speak to each other and not at each other. They saw that communication is very crucial in a marriage or in any relationship dealing with other people. If they had no communication, how could they understand each other or themselves, which include each other's likes and dislikes and the emotions of one another? This is what helps you to have love and concern for your spouse. They also had to learn how to trust each other, because as long as there is no trust, there is no relationship and also, they had to learn how to be there for each other no matter what. So through all of their education, they seemed to be maturing nicely. All married couples have to go through many procedures in order to have a happy, successful marriage and that was one of their goals.

He was triumphantly climbing the ladder of success on his job as an apprentice. Each new ladder he'd climb, his salary also would climb and she continued to work. He was looking forward to his graduation from his apprenticeship program and becoming a journeyman electrician, then he would be producing top dollar. His future was now coming closer to being his present. Life could not have been more abundant for them, they seemed to be living in the beginning of all their dreams except one, and that was to start increasing their family and to have their very own bundle of joy. Ever since they became engaged that was one of their dreams, in fact it was their foremost dream, to start having their family of four children. They could not wait for that day to occur, when they would cradle their baby in their arms, one that was a part of them and their love that they shared and they wanted to share this love with someone else. They felt that they had so much to give.

As the calendar was going forward into days, then weeks, then months and then years, nothing was happening. She could not get pregnant. She was now beginning to worry. She thought maybe something was wrong with one of them. They both decided to see their doctors and have some tests performed to detect what the obstacle was. The doctors could not find anything medically wrong with either of them. The doctors told them to keep trying, and so they did. She felt that during those three years of trying was one of the most frustrating, depressing times of her life. Every month she would wait with anticipation to see if she would be pregnant or not. NOTHING!! She was beginning to think that it would never happen, so she would cry each and every month. It was as if her body was longing to be occupied with that little gift of life. She even went to doctors to have pregnancy tests, just in case. But every time, she heard the same answer, "I'm sorry, you are not pregnant this time. Maybe next time." She was so despondent. In those early years of marriage, they did not know a great deal about God except that He existed and that you called on Him when you were in trouble. They believed that for her to become pregnant it would have to be in His hands. They never realized that she not becoming pregnant was going to carry them both on an adventure that would transport them into a whole new life.

They continued trying to conceive for several years, but to no avail. They felt that they had a considerable measure of love to offer. The majority of their waking hours was filled with the anticipation of them wanting a child. So through considerable discussions, they decided on adoption. They had spoken of the many children in the world that had no family and this couple wanted to share their family with one of them. So the two went to an adoption agency and filled out the necessary paperwork and had various interviews. They were told that there was a two-year waiting list. They were so shattered and so tired of being hopeful. It seemed that this was all they did throughout their former years of marriage and that was to be hopeful that she would get pregnant and if she didn't, they would have to continue waiting for the next month and now they are telling them it was going to be another two years and that just added up to more waiting. They still did not give up but continued trying to get pregnant because they seemed to have all the time in the world. But still nothing. To their amazement, approximately three months later, the agency called and said that they had a little girl for them and that she was only two and a half years old. They were so delighted and so ecstatic, the waiting was finally over and that meant that they were finally going to become parents and that they were, finally, going to have that family that they both dreamed of.

They hurried to get ready her little room that they had fixed for this special day, the day that they would bring home their child to sleep in the room specifically made for her. A few days later, the time had finally come for them to leave and pick up their little girl. They were so nervous because this was one more big move for them. They were going to be responsible not just for himself or herself but now for a little person who was going to depend completely on them.

Questions kept invading their minds, were they ready? I think this is a question and fear of every parent, whether they adopt or have their own, because this is a tremendous responsibility. But they knew that this was a big challenge and one that they could achieve together. Well the time was now, the couple glimpsed across the room and there she was. The three of them fixed their eyes on each other for the very first time. The couple carefully walked across the room to be introduced to their little girl. When she saw them, her face lit up with a gigantic smile. She was so affectionate and that put the couple at ease. After being together for a few minutes, it felt as though this couple had known this child her entire life.

She was quite talkative and asked many questions, nevertheless she was a typical two-year-old and she was quite enthusiastic to depart and to set forth her new beginnings. They brought their little girl to her brand new residence and she made herself very comfortable and at home, it was as if she had been there forever. It was entertaining watching her play with all her new toys and she was so excited that she just bounced from one toy to the other, she had so many to choose from. The couple immediately got into the swing of things. It was as though they were veterans at parenting. Their little girl made it easy because she really did not give them a difficult time in adjusting to her new surroundings. They were ultimately a family... the three of them. This couple was starting to finally experience a sense of satisfaction; their day did not be composed of wanting a child because they now had their child, their little girl. All the fear and anxieties departed and they felt completely blessed.

There were still numerous things they had to discover about child-rearing and being a parent. You have to find out how to be a loving and caring mother and a father, you experience how to share and give all your time to nurturing this young life and showing them the right way to go, and most importantly, lots of love. This little family did everything together, they went everywhere together, and grew closer each and everyday. They paid a visit to family and friends and also traveled to many states and countries together. They were a real family. It seemed as though their dream had come true. While their little girl was entering their life, another Being also started entering as well; He started introducing Himself and that Being was God...

There are so many things about life and what our purpose is that went without answers. Questions that you wanted answers to. The couple would discuss various examples that happened in their life and wondered why. The big question was why they were never able to conceive. With their numerous inquiries, it took him to the book of explanations and so he decided to begin reading the Bible. They had never really done that before and in fact, they did not know anything about the Bible except for some of the popular stories that most of us heard about. He would share with her some of his findings. It was like opening up a treasure chest. It was leading them to God and showing them how loving and powerful He is. As time would push on, more and more knowledge was made understood through the scriptures.

As time passed, she, once again, started to experience emptiness inside of her. Her body began to crave for a child. She could not liberate herself of these feelings no matter how hard she tried. She would feel so guilty about still having that hungering feeling to conceive a baby from her body. Her inner self ached with those empty feelings, and she thought that her feelings were inappropriate and that she should not still be having them. She would ask herself, why should she still be feeling this way? She had this wonderful husband and a beautiful child and she still had these empty and maternal feelings that just would not go away. It wasn't until studying the Bible that she read, "There are things that are never satisfied, the barren womb," see Proverbs 30:15-16. This was her answer and it truly took away the guilt of having these feelings, because God, in His infinite wisdom, understood. This is the way that a woman's body was created, to bear children, and her barrenness was not satisfied. That did not mean that she did not love her little girl, but she could not help her feelings because that was the way that women are made, and their bodies know when that something is missing. Her body hungered for that child. But they knew that God was in their lives, and this just made them closer to God and to each other. What was happening to them was that instead of a child from their bodies entering their lives, there was someone more powerful, a greater Being started to take part in their lives.

Sometimes God will use something that is our heart's desire to capture our attention and to turn us from ourselves and to turn us around to Him. He teaches us that He is the Potter and we are the clay that He is in charge of us all and of all things. Also, that He is our Deliverer, our Redeemer, and our Healer. But there are conditions that we must adhere to and that is, we are to put all our faith and trust in Him. He loves us, He is our Friend and our Dad and in order to recognize this, He has to sometimes get our attention so that we are able to focus on Him. As much as her body hungered for that child, they were both being taught to be appreciative for all that was bestowed upon them and to rely on their God because He was in control of all things. They both have come a long way from January 22, 1972, which was only a few years ago but God now started opening their minds to Him and His truth and also He started giving them life.

They both started traveling through their new discovered life. She a little slower than her husband. She had been a person that did not believe in anything unless she could see it. It was so difficult for her, at times, to understand that God can do anything, that nothing is impossible for Him. But rationally, she could not understand nor see the "how can that be?" But faith you can't see, it is not physical, it is spiritual because God is spiritual. Faith comes from God and it is His gift to us. It took her years to comprehend that one. But God with His patience and wisdom kept holding her hand and He kept right on teaching her.

The three of them, with God's help, continued their journey down the path, a path that led them to helping themselves get to know more about their Creator and His way of life for mankind. The three would sit down for intervals of time and just talk about God and all that He has done for them and then they would open the bible and have studies.

They wanted to bring up their little girl to know her Father and to know He is there for her no matter what problems may arise, and more importantly, that He loved her. It truly was a captivating travel, because in God's eyes, the three of them, no matter what the age, were His little babies and He would show them each day, something that required them to depend solely on Him. They started with taking baby steps. It is like a little baby that is learning to walk, the parent will hold the hand of the child while the baby learns to take his or her first steps. The parent would not let go until they knew the child was fully capable to stand on his own two feet and then the parent would hold out their hands until the child would walk right into their arms. That child knew that their parent would not let them hurt themselves. That child learned to trust their parents and that is what we must learn to do, to trust our parent, who is God Almighty. He was teaching them that He really loved them and that He could do all! He was teaching them how to have faith. Like what was said in previous pages, God used something that was their heart's desire, and that was a baby and He was bringing them to something that was far greater, Him.

God truly brought them closer together each day as a family, because this was an experience that they all shared in. They saw people around them having family problems, financial problems, all kinds of horrendous problems, and these people were suffering without hope, because they did not know that there was someone who was far greater than any man, which can take us out of any problem or problems. Not that this family did not have problems, but they knew that they could put their burdens on His shoulders and also put it in His hands, and He would help them solve whatever the problem was, every time. But God never tells us when or how He will help us, so another lesson we must learn and that is patience. Practicing patience is not an easy task, in fact, it is very difficult because we humans want things yesterday. Remember this, faith produces patience.

She still had those dissatisfying feelings of not becoming pregnant, but now it was not as severe. God was teaching her to put it in His hands and that He would take care of it. God teaches us about Him through our trials. He will start with something small, just enough to get our attention and then He will let us know who is in charge and they certainly had their share of trials. Their biggest one was financial troubles. As you know her husband is in the construction field and there were times that he'd be out of work because there would be a scarcity of jobs. But they were always taken care of, and the reason was, because God was teaching them that He was there Provider. At the right time, her husband would go back to work and things would start looking up. God was teaching them that they were His students and that they would begin in the first grade and when you would pass that assignment, you can have no doubt that you would be promoted to the next level. At each promotion, the trials would get a little harder and He would not answer you as rapidly as He did in the earlier grades. There were times you wanted to drop out but He would be there helping you along. He is such a loving, patient Teacher. They would mess up quite often, but He would forgive them and they would go on.

It is so awesome coming to know our wonderful Creator. The All-powerful, Almighty Being, the Maker of all things. How breathtaking! They were in a process of unlearning the wrong ways of life and committing to the right ways. It was all a growing process.

CHAPTER TWO
God Knows Best

We are now into eight years of their fairytale wedding, which brings us up to the year 1980. Employment for her husband in his construction field was not reliable and he was now laid off. This layoff was promised to be a long duration. They all contemplated on a decision on what they should do. She was no longer working because she wanted to stay home and raise their daughter. They had no concept on what they should do, because it looked like there was not going to be employment for sometime. They noticed jobs in the other states were doing better than the state they lived in, which was New York. So they decided to have a family conference to determine on what they should do.

Her husband had two brothers who chose to move out of the state for employment purposes and that helped to make their decision a little easier. But they did not want to make any final agreement until they went to God to see if this was a beneficial action. Her husband spoke to his brother to see how employment was in the state of Illinois where he lived. He informed them there was an abundance of labor. So they decided, Illinois here we come. This was an enormous step for the three of them because this would be the first time that they ever moved out of the state, but it helped to know that family would be there with them.

So here they were the three of them, packing up all their belongings and getting ready to depart to a place they knew nothing about. After realizing that their decision was now about to become a reality, they became so unhappy because they knew they were leaving behind parents, family, friends, and a place they grew up in and appreciated and then to embark on an area, sight unseen. They really knew they needed God with them on this one because they were scared to death.

Well, the time had come to say their good-byes. It was one of the most painful things they had to do. It felt as though someone near and dear to them had died. They had no notion how long they would be gone, but they knew they would someday return, back home again. They kissed all that came to see their departure and got in the car and took one last look at everyone and all their familiar surroundings and off they drove, the three of them, crying their eyes out. She cried all the way to Pennsylvania. But they knew it was something that they had to do.

After much driving, they finally entered the state of Illinois. It was definitely different from where they came from. They could see right away that the pace was much slower and they felt they could get use to this. They still had quite a long drive in the state, to the small town they would be living in. The further they drove along the highway; they could see nothing but corn and wheat fields. The only thing they knew about farm products was what you purchase in the grocery store. This was truly a culture shock, a far cry from New York! They finally reached their town. They knew it was small, but not this small, with a population of 18,000 people. Leaving a city with millions and moving to a town with less than twenty thousand, she suddenly became very homesick. To help them not to think of the sad memories that they left behind, they said that they would make this into a new adventure and tried to find the positive side of all of this.

While being there for sometime, they soon adapted to living away from the Big Apple and they all agreed that this new adventure of theirs was not that regretful. They started making new friends in the neighborhood, her husband met all sorts of people from all over the United States on his job and their daughter got to meet some people from school that actually lived on farms.

One day, she had a little frightening moment. She was home watching television and her husband was at work and their daughter was at school. To her shock, while watching TV, there on the screen appeared a special weather bulletin. They had issued a tornado warning for their neighborhood. She was somewhat concerned because she did not know the first thing of what to do in case of a tornado. In fact, she was terrified to death. Here she was from New York and the only bad weather she was use to were snowstorms and maybe a hurricane, but nothing really significant like this. She wondered what should she do? The only thing she knew to do was call her mother back in New York, who also never lived anywhere else but New York and here she was asking her what to do? Her mother, also, didn't have a clue on what to do in a tornado.

Meanwhile, the wind starting blowing up a little and then it started gusting and it very dark outside. She hurried to hang up the phone, and not only was she scared to death, but now she made her mother scared to death, as well. The only thing she did know to do was pray and ask God to please let this tornado pass over this town, because she was home alone and was about to panic. Guess what happened? The hand of God spared them and this tornado passed right over their town. After that, she questioned the neighbors and asked what to do in case of a tornado emergency. The neighbors instructed them on how to look at the skies and to observe how the clouds form when a tornado is approaching. They did get to experience two tornadoes while living there. One time, they were outside and barely made it into the house, it was like the *Wizard of Oz* and another time, her husband was in the car in front of the house and all of a sudden it became so dark and this huge gust of wind came and actually lifted one side of the car slightly while he was in there. It wasn't fun at the time, but after, it was actually a roller coaster adventure. They envied their daughter slightly, because she was now eight years old and she was obtaining a great and wonderful education, one that would carry her through to her adult life. This was an astonishing time of their lives, one that seemed so dismal in the beginning, but was turning into a great challenging experience for the three of them. They were, indeed, seeing another form of the hand of God and how He is in control.

I will inform you that this couple was learning how to derive joy from a changed style of living, a manner in which they were not accustomed. This new adventure was one that they had to grow to appreciate, because all of this was really unique for them. A couple they were introduced to, who became one of their closest friends, lived on a farm. It was a milking farm, primarily. They also had some cattle that they slaughtered for food. The three of them being from the "big city" only saw a cow from the car, as they drove by on the highway. But here they were on a milking farm and became face to face with, to them, one of God's largest animals and they were so near. The farmers brought the cows into the barn, all lined up one by one and placed each one carefully behind the other as they attached these milking implements to every cow and guess what happened, here came the milk. Fresh, creamy milk. This was one of the greatest things to watch. It showed them how every living creature has a meaning and a reason for their existence. This farm also included some chickens, horses and sheep.

Their daughter also learned how to feed a calf with a baby bottle, and also she fed the chickens. It was funny to see the chickens flap about and sometimes they would run after her which started to become a game for her and the chickens. She was also, encountering how not to be afraid of these animals, a far cry from her parents, who in the beginning, were somewhere huddled in a corner until coaxed out by their friends. This was another way of existing about with the rest of

God's creation. They also had an appreciation for all the laborious work that farmers have to perform, so that we all have food to eat. It showed them not to always take things for granted, to look deeper than what the eye can see. When God says, "in toil that man is to eat. Both thorns and thistle it shall bring forth. By the sweat of your face you shall eat bread" (Gen. 3:17-18). That is precisely how hard these farmers had to work, from sun up to sun down.

After watching the farmers carrying out their daily responsibilities, they all decided they would proceed in for dinner. They were served an assortment of fresh foods from the garden and also farm-fresh steak, one that was slaughtered from their multitude of cattle. The three had a difficult time swallowing the steak, knowing that once it was alive, running around, grazing in the grass and now they had to eat the poor thing. But after many tries without choking, they were able to swallow and enjoy the steak; it was so tender and juicy. She knew the next time she would go into a grocery store that she would have great respect of how the meat got in the containers.

What seemed like a dismal decision they had made by moving from New York to a small town, that appeared to have nothing to offer, was turning into place that taught them more than most "city folk" would ever learn about which is really important, also it gave an education that a lot of colleges don't offer and that is, real hands on experience about life in God's world. This was something that they would have never received, if they did not let God lead them in the decision, about their moving to Illinois. The day was about to wind up, and it was time for them to leave and go back to their small town. They left with many memories and also fresh eggs from the chickens, and they could not wait until their next visit, which would give them more to store in their memory bank.

The ride back to their small town was approximately sixty miles. One thing they learned living in the country is that mileage means nothing, because everything was so remote. But what is great about living in the rural area, there is absolutely no traffic, none at all. The roads are wide open, with lots of space and farmland. The land is so flat, that you could view as far as the eye would allow. The three of them would just sing and play games on their travels to and fro, on these rustic roads. So sixty miles took no time at all, to arrive home. It was such a beautiful and a fun filled day, one that they will never overlook.

They have been in Illinois for exactly one and a half years. Her husband got news that employment had picked up tremendously in New York. They knew that their trip to Illinois was only a temporary one and that one-day they would return back to New York. So the time had come, it was time to head home. They had much sadness in their hearts, knowing that they were going to leave so many good friends behind. They knew that this year and a half were something that they would cherish for the rest of their lives. But like some things in our lives, this was another change, and a new adventure, one that they had to let God lead them in, and guide them down another new road. So again, they packed their belongings and prepared for another trip, this time to a place they knew, to a place they missed, to people they longed to see; but still they had to leave a place, they had grown to love, friends that became family to them and so again, with many tears falling from their eyes, this was another good-bye that they had to repeat. So away they went, and as they waved good-bye, they knew they were leaving to return back home, back to New York.

This time the move was a little different. They rented a moving truck and relocated their own furniture. He drove the truck and she drove the car with their little girl. They took their long travel, approximately one thousand miles, and headed home. It was an exhausting trip because they did not have each other to assist with the driving, so each was on his and her own. But not really because they had God as their co-pilot. As they were driving, they noticed something that brought a shiver up their spine, that famous sign that read... entering New York!!! Things appeared to be quite different. Being away for a year and a half, they had some things to get use to, the heavy traffic, the many people and everyone wanted to get there, yesterday. The sign should have read, "Welcome Home!" They soon adapted to the fast pace, and they were happy to be back home. They could not wait to get through the traffic, to get home to see their family and friends that they had not seen in awhile. They were feeling a little emotional of what they left behind but they would never forget their memories of Illinois, and all the enlightenment they experienced, that they would hold dear in their hearts for the rest of their lives.

Well here they were, driving their large truck and car into her parent's driveway. This is where they would remain until they were able to find someplace to live. Everyone was so elated to see each other. It felt as though they had been away for a long time. They immediately got back into the swing of things. Her husband promptly went back to work and their little girl went back to school. Her job seemed to be the most difficult; she had to find a suitable place for them to live. Prices had skyrocketed in just that short period of time they were gone. They had forgotten how expensive it was living in New York. She saw several places that they would have grabbed, but some difficulty would arise and they would not take it. But they patiently kept right on looking, but to no avail. They thought they would only be at her parent's home, for a couple of weeks, but now their stay was turning into months. They were invading her parent's space, but they could not find anywhere to live. They started wondering if it was a mistake coming back to New York, because in this big city, how could only three people not find anywhere to live.

A friend of theirs notified them about this house on Long Island and that the previous family that lived in the house was moving, and the house would be vacant in a few weeks. They did not especially want to live on Long Island; their dream was to live upstate New York. It appeared to be lovely in that area of the state. So, the search was on and they continued to search for that dream house upstate.

And then at last... there it was... their dream house! It was gorgeous. The three of them just simply fell in love with this house. It had three bathrooms, one for each of them, two terraces, three bedrooms, a lovely living room, dining room and a huge kitchen. One terrace was connected to the master bedroom and the other was connected to the dining room. She started to picture them having breakfast while sitting on their terrace. It was impressive. Their attitude became; "we have to have this house, NOW!" They were so eager that they could not wait to start proceedings.

Bright and early the next morning, they went to the bank to apply for the mortgage. It was a little frightening, once they realized that this could be their home and they would own it. The price was a little costly, but this was their dream house and they really wanted it and so they decided that they could do this. So they went on and filled out all the necessary paperwork.

Weeks went by and they had not heard from the bank and they started getting a little impatient. They wondered, what could be the problem? Then finally, the phone call came, and the representative from the bank said, "the loan is yours." Those words sounded like music to their ears, their dream house was now going to be theirs. So they jumped into their car and went to the bank to find out what the next procedure would be. The representative came out expressing regret, by telling them that there was an obstacle preventing them from obtaining the loan and that was that they needed a co-signer. Their heart sank straight to the ground. They were so disappointed, because after much searching they had finally found their dream home and there was a problem. Now what should they do, start all over again looking one more time for another dream house, which could take another long period of time? They could not stay at her parent's house forever. The bank representative saw the disappointment on their faces and told them that he would try to work something out for them. So they left with a little more hope. They decided to go home and put this entire situation in God's hands and they had to come to the conclusion that this had to be in God's hands because it all had to be His will and not theirs. Working with the bank was like watching a tennis match. The ball kept going from one side to the other. One minute they would have the loan and the next minute some other problem would come up. It was too exhausting for them. They did not know what to do. Was God trying to tell them something? They wondered if this house was for them or not? The answer was beginning to look like, "not." They were really disappointed but they put their house hunting into the hands of God, so that He would direct them to the house that He wanted them to have. We must always keep in mind that faith produces patience.

They were now at her parent's house for three months. They were beginning to become frantic. They started searching desperately and were taken to places that were not fit for animals to live in, much less humans. Panic started developing, they needed their own home. Their friend again reminded them of the house on Long Island and by this time it had been vacant for one month and a half. They had no alternative but to go and look at the house on Long Island. As they drove through the neighborhood to the house, they noticed how pleasant and serene it was. The house was located in an area in which everything you would want was not far away. They reached the house and decided to go in. They saw that the house had plenty to offer and that it had things in it that they desired in a home. The house had a big backyard, a large garage, and the back door that led to the backyard, a finished basement, and a den for her husband and all the necessities. This was not so unpleasant after all. They believed that this is where God wanted them to be. The price was more affordable and it was really nice. Here they were again, off to fill out more paperwork. Guess what, this time everything went through smooth as silk and with no problems at all. God came through for them once again and they were now departing her parents home to arrive, finally, in their own home on Long Island.

As they drove up to their new home, they got out and swiftly entered their new residence. The three just stood there and stared. After many months of searching day and night, they were finally home. They were really eager and couldn't wait to start unpacking. You don't realize how many items that you have accumulated, until you move. Thankfully, her husband's brother was there to assist, because they had many heavy pieces of furniture. The men started bringing in the large, heavy items, while she and her daughter brought in the lighter things.

After many hours of strenuous work, it was finally finished and they were unpacked. Her husband and his brother went and returned the truck and she and her daughter tried to gather some food to eat. They were all so tired, but it was a good tired. This was their first night in their new home and they all were so weak from fatigue that they could barely keep their eyes open and for that reason, they had an excellent nights sleep.

The next day, as they started to find a spot for various things, they went into the basement to further explore what was there. God will rescue us when we place our troubles into His hands and He will, also, let you know when He answers your prayers. Her husband had always prayed to have a house that would allow him to have his own study, with a bulletin board, desk and file cabinets. As they were in the basement cleaning, they located something in a corner that had a sheet across it. They went over to it and started taking off the sheet, and guess what was underneath, that's right, his bulletin board, his desk and his two file cabinets. All what he had prayed for was now staring them in the face. So right then and there, they were confident what their answer from God was, they knew that this is where He wanted them to live, in this house, on Long Island. We think that our will is a priority over God's will, but as you can see, the answer they got for upstate was definitely a no. God knows best and He knows our past, present and future. That is why He has to guide us, because we do not know what our future holds. The Bible says, "that all things work together for good to those who love God" (Rom. 8:28). As this book continues, you will see how that scripture applies to this family and to all of us.

The three were so happy to be capable of accomplishing some repairs and to brighten their new home with their individual characteristics. They were trying to make their house feel like a home of hospitality. It was so much fun. Their little girl was having a good time adding her touch to her very own room. Her room represented her interior decorating skills, with all her belongings and her memories of some of the places they had visited while traveling to various sites.

Their daughter rapidly made some friends in the neighborhood. She enjoyed playing with them in her very own backyard. They still missed their friends in Illinois, but they knew that this place was home for them. It was a big adjustment for them, moving from the City of New York, to Illinois and now to Long Island. But this time it would be more lasting. They would start right here, in this very house, to have the adventure of their lives.

The days were marching forward and life was back to being routine for them. Her husband was back to work and their little girl was in her new school. She was in one of the best school districts in New York. This school had so much to present. She had advanced academic subjects, she learned the computer, and she learned to play several instruments and also became active in various school activities. She also made new friends and she loved her new school very much. The three of them were very contented in their new home and they were so thankful to God for sending them to Long Island. They knew that He always knows best.

Winter was approaching and they had to buy winter supplies for outside work. Here it was their first snowflake! That year they had a fierce snowstorm and so they all went outside to shovel. After their lengthy fatiguing performance of shoveling the snow, they decided to have some fun and make a snowman, which they named Alfred. They created this snowman with rocks for his eyes, nose and mouth, some sticks for his arms, some bottle caps for his buttons and they put a hat and a scarf on him and when he was finished, and he looked like Frosty the Snowman. After their creation, they decided to have a snowball fight the two girls against the one boy. Even though there were two against one, he still won. He knew just how to form those big snowballs really fast and they traveled with such speed and theirs just fell apart while sailing through the air, they started laughing so hard. They started becoming conscious of how cold it was and thought they'd better go inside before they got frost bitten. They really enjoyed their very first winter, but now the spring season was soon making its entrance.

They couldn't wait to begin planting their first garden and to be competent enough to use some of the educational skills they had received while living in Illinois. As the season was approaching, they bought some fertilizer and supplies to start their digging for their garden. Her husband went out and chose a spot that received plenty of sunlight and then he proceeded to dig. This was really toilsome work. What was stated previously, they had learned to have a great deal of high regard for the farmers and how their job is so difficult. The ground was now completed and prepared for planting. So the three went shopping to choose their vegetables that they wanted to grow. They decided on some lettuce, cucumbers, tomatoes, green peppers, carrots, and some string beans. They thought that this was adequate for amateurs. Her husband did plenty of reading to learn exactly how to plant and what flowers were good to keep the bugs away. Here they were again, with another family undertaking which they were all going to reap whatever they would sow. Following the planting, they watered the vegetation and then they prayed that God would bless what they have now sown. Everyday the three of them would go outside to see if anything green was peeking through the soil. They knew that it would not occur that quickly, but just in case, they did not want to miss a thing. Every day each would take turns watering when necessary and then one day, there it was, they spotted something green peeking through the soil. They were so excited that they started jumping up and down for joy. As the days rolled by, the plants continued to grow.

At least once a week, they would have to remove the weeds and the plants were looking so robust, and then came the next step, they started to see the vegetables appearing on the plants. This was it; success started ringing in their ears. They knew that they were that much closer to eating their own vegetables from their first harvest. They had also added to their landscaping some beautiful flowers that were placed around their house. They, too, were growing and were starting to bloom. Everything was looking marvelous, and the smell of the flowers filled the air.

They couldn't wait for summer to get there, because they had been planning their first barbecue ever since the winter. The first year in their new home was the greatest. They had a great deal of fun. They, also, had an abundant amount of people visiting and all relished in the enjoyment of their home. Their little girl was growing nicely and she, too, kept quite active with various summer activities. There was a pool in the neighborhood, so the little one took swimming lessons and learned how to swim. Nothing but blessings seemed to be coming their way since they moved to Long Island.

Time was up; their vegetables were now ready for picking. Freshly grown garden vegetables cannot stack up against what you buy in the supermarkets. The freshly grown just melts in your mouth and it even had a different taste. It was so delicious that their daughter even had a great appreciation for eating her vegetables and for her to know that she had a part in the preparation of its growing process. God was truly blessing this family and they felt Him so close to them.

Summer started departing and fall started entering and something started happening. It was going to be a time that they would awaken from their peaceful way of life, to one that could be considered a life of turbulence. Cinderella and her Prince Charming were about to awaken from their dream-filled lifestyle, to one that was going to seem like one big continuous nightmare.

CHAPTER THREE
Believe in the Promises

We are now going to move backward several years, to the time of 1969. This, of course, was before they had gotten married. In fact, it was shortly after they first met, when they were beginning their friendship. He had been having unusual difficulties with his eyes, they were continually watering and they would readily turn red. He kept going back and forth to physicians, but they did not discover any solution to his problems. They presumed it was his vision and they had given him eyeglasses, but he had 20/20 vision. He continued going to different specialists to see if they would diagnose what his problem was.

One day, he discovered a doctor who took a series of tests and detected that the pressure was high in his eyes. He was diagnosed with glaucoma. Glaucoma generally attacked people when they got older, it was an elderly person's disease and, also, there is no cure for it, but yet controllable. The doctor prescribed medication for him to use in his eyes every day. He was instructed to use the eye drops three times a day, which he would faithfully do. He would have to see the doctor once a month, sometimes twice, to exam his eye pressure and vision and to make sure there was no vision loss. The doctors informed him that his medication was not working, because his pressure was getting higher and higher, however his vision seemed to remain the same, 20/20. The doctor decided to prescribe a stronger dosage of eye drops and also some pills that were to aid in bringing the pressure down. They, too, were not working the way the doctor had hoped, but her husband kept taking the medication and he was, also, suffering a few side effects. There were times when he did not feel well and would get a little dizzy, in addition to, walking around with blurry vision that sometimes restricted him from doing particular errands, along with performing his job accurately. The doctors even spoke of doing some surgery to bring down the pressure and that was not an infallible guarantee. During these months, when he was discovering about his eye problems, they had become boyfriend and girlfriend and in fact, they were engaged at this time.

Before they got married, they didn't preoccupy themselves with the glaucoma that he suffered because it really was no big deal and he would just take his medication and learned how to handle the side effects. It was not until after they got married, that the eye problems appeared to get worse. Let's not overlook, since their wedding day they still had the sorrow of not being able to receive their very own baby, nevertheless at this time, it was his glaucoma that was getting out of control. The doctors worked diligently to bring the fluctuating pressure to stability and he continued to take what they prescribed, but he knew there had to be a better way. She did not know that he had taken his illness to God. Remember what I said previously, that God had used the problem of them not receiving their very own child, to introduce them to Him, and now, they learned that one more problem has entered their life, and they knew that this one, likewise, had to be in the hands of God.

He would study the Bible daily and he prayed that God would lead him in the right direction, by way of his studies. He was led to a subject that seemed to fascinate him greatly which was the topic about faith, the promises of God and the assurances God would carry out IF we obeyed Him. He came to the scriptures that said, "Who forgives all your iniquities" and "Who heals all your diseases" (Ps. 103); also, "I am the

Lord that heals you" (Ex. 15); also, "I will take sickness away from the midst of you" (Ex.23). This is just to name a few of God's promises to heal. She and her husband saw in God's Word, that we have a God that heals. So he decided to go to his Creator, his Healer. He would put it all in His hands.

In the Bible, it also says, "is anyone among you sick? Let him call for the elders of the church and let them pray over you, anointing you with oil in the name of the Lord, and the prayer of faith will save the sick, and the Lord will raise him up" (James 5:14-15). So her husband went to the elders of the church and was anointed, and then he decided to put it entirely in God's hands and to trust Him. This decision was made in the year 1978.

As time continued to proceed ahead, they both grew stronger each day in faith, through prayer and fasting. God became more and more actual in their lives and was, also, becoming closer to each of them. One of the most priceless gifts that God could give an individual is the gift of faith and theirs was about to be literally tested.

We are, at this time, in the year 1981... Her husband woke up early one morning to prepare for work and that is when he initially noticed a blind spot, right in the center of his vision. With the disease of glaucoma, people ordinarily begin losing their peripheral vision, but he started right in the center of his vision. When he informed her of his first blind spot, she became slightly nervous because the foremost thought that came to her mind was that he would be shattered, thinking that God had let him down and then, next, she thought that prior to his first blind spot that it was so much easier to believe that God would heal him, because he had 20/20 vision, but now, he has a blind spot and the awareness started to set in, that he could really go blind. But instead of him becoming insecure in his belief that God would heal him, he became stronger than ever and was determined to trust in the one true God. His strength is what held her and their little girl together and so, they in turn were able to become stronger. Yet, through his beginnings of losing sight, he was still fully capable to drive and go to work. Life continued along as expected.

As the months and years marched forward, his eyesight was progressively getting worse. He was, nevertheless, still able to drive and continued working, but it was getting increasingly more complex for him to perform his job, considering he was an electrician, but life continued to move along smoothly and peacefully and that is precisely what God was doing, He was allowing his working skills to continue to go along peacefully, until it was time for him to discontinue working. By the year 1983, he had become legally blind and that year was one of the toughest periods of life's unpredictable changes for him, because he now was being faced with making an exceptionally huge decision. It was now time for him to relinquish his job and his driving, and for him, that was like giving up his independence. Now they were faced with the question, "now what do we do?"

God was once again bringing them into another educational level and that was; they now had to learn to depend solely on Him. She thought to herself, maybe she had to reenter the work force and provide for the family; but that was not an easy decision, because her husband was now facing one of the biggest challenges of his life, and she could not abandon him at this crucial time. The year 1983 was about to be one of the most distressing trials of their lives, for the three of them. They had to learn to depend solely on a Being they were just establishing a relationship with and also, one they could not see or hear.

Life was beginning to become burdensome for the three. Her husband, who was always a creditable provider for his family and one that they always depended on, was now facing the toughest battle of his life, no eyesight, no job and no

40

money. They were so frightened because they did not know what to do. All sorts of emotions were building up inside of them and at times problems would become so overwhelming, that they felt as though they would not be able to deal with them. They had to go to God and beseech Him for guidance and strength in order to be able to manage this.

Her husband had to apply for disability insurance. They were informed that it would take sometime before any money would commence. In the meantime, obligations had to be paid. They had to eat, they had to have a roof over their heads, they had to care for a growing child and they had to pay bills. But where was the money going to come from? She, again, was forced to contemplate the concept of going back to work, but when she examined the circumstances of what was happening to her family, she knew that she was needed at home, to assist with the afflictions they were now experiencing.

They prayed and asked God to help, to lead, and to guide them and that they would understand what direction to take. Their life, indeed, got turbulent. There were instances when they did not have heat in the house because they didn't have the money for oil and so they would purchase kerosene for their kerosene heater and remain in one room for warmth. There were circumstances when it seemed as if they would not have food to eat, but someone always would invite them for dinner, not knowing their situation, or else someone would bring them food. God was moving minds because not once did they complain to others or express anything about what they were going through, because they knew that this was between them and God and they did not want anyone to get the impression that it was wrong to trust God, or that He would simply abandon them in time of need, nevertheless, they were confident that He didn't.

There was a time, when their daughter outgrew some of her clothing and people would offer her quality outfits, some were brand new and some were hand-me-downs; but she was decked like a princess. They in no way got angry at God or blamed Him for anything, because they knew He led them to these findings, just like He led them to their house, and, also, that He was alongside them. They did not understand why they were going through these sore trials nor why He would take them so far without deliverance, but they did know that He was with them, right there holding their hand and giving them strength; that much they did know.

Every once in a while, God would reveal to them that He was among them. This time He created a miracle for them, one that would encourage them to increase their strength in their convictions. One day, their cesspool was full and it started backing up all over their basement floor. They had no money to have it fixed and they did not want to go to anyone for help, because they felt this was their responsibility. It had nothing to do with pride, but they knew that the decision they made was, just that, their decision and they had to be the ones to handle their problems alone with their God. That day of the backup, she was so depressed and she decided to visit a friend. He stayed home trying so hard to clear the cesspool himself, but to no avail. Despair started setting it, because he did not know what he was going to do. They could not use any water at all, which also meant that they could not even go to the bathroom. How long does it have to take, until we humans decide to go to the accurate specialist for assistance.

God tells us to cast our worries on Him and Him alone. Hence, he finally realized that he could not do this alone. While he was still in the basement, standing there staring down the water filled pipe, is when he cried out to God for His intervention. All of a sudden, he heard a rumble and then with the limited vision he had, he saw the cesspool, which was filled to the top become unobstructed of nasty, smelly water, with the help of God. During the time that he was there for hours trying to unclog the cesspool by himself, absolutely nothing happened, but with the help of God it only took minutes and with victory. Things that seem impossible become possible with God. He showed them that He was there with them every step of the way. God was strengthening their faith every single day. God wants us to depend on Him solely. Yes, there were plenty of times that they were afraid and became very depressed, but they would go to the Bible and let God encourage them. One of her favorite scriptures is, "all things, whatever you ask in prayer, believing, you will receive" (Matt.21:22). This is the scripture that would continue to echo in her ears, through her present and yet future trials. These words became an important ingredient of her strength.

The Bible is complete with people, just like you and I, and you can journey through it and discover someone that has gone through related troubles and they can encourage you and strengthen you through whatever trouble you may be going through. Their choice, at this specific time, was King David. David went through some severe trials, but whatever the situation, he learned to trust God. You can read the book of Psalms and see how David cried out to God and said, "the righteous cry out and the Lord hears, and delivers him out of all their troubles" (Ps. 34:17); also, he said, "many are the afflictions of the righteous, but the Lord delivers him out of them all" (vs. 19). These were some of the scriptures that were added with the others and, these too, they held on to each and every day.

God did redeem them from their economic anguish. His disability payments started a year later and God also blessed her with some clerical work that she was able to perform from home, so that she could be there with her husband during these troublesome times. It never fails, God doesn't hold back on His promises.

As time kept moving onward, his eyesight continued to get progressively worse. He was losing more and more of his independence but was growing more and more in his dependence on God. Anyone that has gone through any drastic change in their live, can understand the challenges that arrive with the changes, not only did he lose his eyesight but he also started losing himself; and so, additional problems shortly followed. You have a man, that is young and that had so many dreams but not the ones that seemed to have been assigned to him, so he began to feel like he was losing everything in the process. He had to confront with so many emotional and mental pressures. He had to examine precisely who he was and what he had become. He had to reevaluate all the decisions that he had made, if they were the correct solutions for him and his family, also, he would have to listen to individuals who may condemn him. He felt as though he had no self-value, no self-confidence and, at times, he felt all alone. There were some mental disabilities that went along with the physical disabilities, particularly when people may utter or believe that he did this to himself.

But he soon discovered that he was not alone, unless he chose to be alone. God always disclosed to him that He was there no matter what and no matter how people would make him feel. God demonstrated that He would not leave him and with that consolation, it encouraged him not to have remorse over the decisions he made, no matter what anyone thought or said, because he never lost hope of the promises that God made. This shaped the three of them into a stronger family, because thus far, they have been through plenty and have lost a great deal. She and their daughter stood behind him one hundred percent, because they believed God was with them and that they would not be alone, no matter what was ahead for them.

She taught her daughter that life was similar to a new book and while you are absorbing knowledge, you would travel from page to page and chapter to chapter, not knowing what would be on the other side of each page, and then the next chapter would bring a whole new discovery. Well life, for the three of them, was a new discovery and with each new page they would unquestionably set foot into a new chapter, one that the three of them did not know what would be bound for their destination. You never know how long God will try you, but with one conclusion, the only conclusion, is not to give up. As the adage asks, "how do you look at a half glass of water, do you view it as half empty or half full?" We must learn to look at it as half full, because God says "He will never leave us or forsake us" (Heb. 13:5), no matter what. We must meditate on the positive and not the negative because God is not negative, but we humans sometimes are.

Yes, what was spoken previously, they did feel broken hearted and there were times when they felt like all of their strong beliefs and all of their waiting were performed in vain, and it also felt like they were in a predicament that looked hopeless; because here they were, the three, looking to God, to number one, give them a baby from her body and also, number two, to give back to this man his eyesight; now logically thinking, that indeed seemed impossible. Yes, there was a period when they both wanted to give up and throw in the towel, to run away from this life that was handed to them. Their body ached for deliverance from God. They would beg, "why them?"

Her heart ached, when she watched him struggling to make it through the day and on to the following day and she trying not to become discouraged. To watch him each and every day, with his eyesight continuing to get worse and merely a few years later, he went from legally blind to totally blind. She would conceal herself from him and just take off and allow the tears to just stream down her cheeks. She thought she had no one that she could talk to, that could understand and not criticize. She needed encouragement and not discouragement. How much longer did they have to go through this? They were still so young, only in their early thirties, they felt as though they had lost so much. "Dear God," her insides would scream, "how much longer?" This song that she heard, really hit close to home; it was a song that encouraged her during these trying times. The song went like this,

"When you walk through a storm,
Hold your head up high
And don't be afraid of the dark,
Cause at the end of the storm,
There's a golden sky,
· And the sweet silver song of a lark.
Walk on through the wind,
Walk on through the rain,
Though your dreams may be tossed and blown.
Walk on with hope in your heart,
And you'll never walk alone."

She knew that God loved them more than they could ever love each other, because He is the author of love, and the giver of it. She knew that God had a written Book of promises, promises that she knew that He would not break and she would hold Him to those promises. She realized that God knew best and this would have to be left to Him. They could not fail Him or themselves, they would have to continue, and they could, with God's help.

Let's again go over the lessons this family was taught. God started teaching them about faith with them wanting a baby and to never let go of their heart's desire and that hope, as you know, never departed from them. One more time, let's go back to the Bible and let's meet some new friends that also went through resembling obstacles. Their names are Abraham and Sarah. This was a couple that also desired to have a baby and they too had to patiently wait on God. Now he was 100 years old and she was 90 when they ultimately had their baby, Isaac. They never gave up believing that God would grant them their baby. How do I know? Because the Bible said, "that Abraham believed God, he (Abraham) did not waver at the promises of God through unbelief, but was strengthened in faith, giving glory to God, and being fully convinced that what God had promised, He was able to perform" (Rom. 4:20-21). You see, God can do all things and nothing can stop Him, not even age when it came to Him giving them their very own son, so, we too, must not ever lose hope. Oh yes, at times, it is very hard, but no one promised, it would be effortless. In fact, when you look in the Bible, you see that no one had it easygoing; but remember that hope does not disappoint. So this family clung to the story of Abraham and Sarah as their incentive, when it came to them receiving that child from their body was granted by God, because they, too, believed. I know that Abraham and Sarah did not anticipate being 100 and 90 years old, but God promised, they believed and God delivered. He never breaks a promise and He does not lie. Take time and study the promises of God.

You will be so surprised to see how many there are. Go to Him in prayer and look to receive answers from Him and then believe and also trust Him to fulfill them. But also remember, human nature wants the answer and deliverance from God, immediately, as soon as we request, but He doesn't always tell us when it will happen, and also, there are things that we must do, we must obey His commands given to us. He is a great Teacher and He truly wants us all to be His students. The class may be stormy and bumpy at times, but anything worthwhile receiving is never easy, and when you receive it, you will surely be thankful.

CHAPTER FOUR
Love Casts out All Fear

There were many times that she would reminisce about the past, before they both got married. She would call to mind all the goals they had laid for themselves, their expectations of married life and their dreams of what they wanted to achieve during their years. It seemed like centuries ago, when they both planned their fairy tale wedding. She glanced over these eleven years of marriage, from 1972 to 1983 and saw all their dreams they both had and hoped for come crumbling down to nonexistence. This was not what they wanted for each other. Notice the operative word, what *they* wanted. There were times, which yes, they would feel so sorry for themselves and they hated life and yes even the worse, there were times they didn't even want to wake up in the morning. There were days they would become so paranoid, that they looked for something unpleasant to occur because of all that was happening to them in their life and they even wondered what they were doing wrong. How can one family go through so much? But then, this incredible strength would come over the three, and they were able to keep right on going, in regard to their every day responsibilities, and with a smile no less. God tells us in His word, "that through our weaknesses, He will give us His strength", and He did and He does.

What I brought up in the preceding chapter, God proceeded to seize them from their financial troubles. They began paying the complete remainder of all their bills that they compiled and also had a small savings account and not to forget, how God blessed her with a job that she was able to perform from their home. Things were beginning to look up for them financially; they were even able to assist others that were going through their financial woes.

When he had first stopped working because of his disability, and it was therefore upsetting financially, they had to sell some of their jewelry in order to make ends meet, and with God's blessing, He bestowed upon them all new jewelry and even blessed them with more than they had before. They were even able to finally repair some of the maintenance that was necessary in the house. God really started to bless them in the early to mid 1980s. He even restored their credit, which was ruined. They were even able to purchase a brand new car. You realize, when you look back on what this family had been through, they always had their home, they always had their transportation, they always had food on the table and they always had clothes on their backs. Their needs were always provided for. God was always carrying them through the storm and they were protected in the safety of His arms.

The three of them were leaving to travel on one of their annual family trips, when they would journey to different sections of the world. This time, they went to one of the tropical islands of Jamaica in the year of 1987. They felt so blessed to be able to go somewhere that was so relaxing and all they had to do was to lie on the enjoyable beaches and watch the waves come in and go out. How superb! They had gone with a few of their friends and one of their biggest enjoyments was the happy hour and the Caribbean entertainment. This particular evening, their daughter and a few friends had entered one of the hotel's amateur contests. They chose to sing a song. They didn't win, but in spite of that; they didn't sound that shabby. It was completely entertaining and everyone seemed to be having lots of fun.

Subsequent to relaxing and enjoying the tropical sun of the

island, they went to church. While they were sitting in church, it had become quite heated and it was also very muggy that day and the air conditioning was not applicable and she began feeling slightly woozy in her head. She started to experience a weak feeling and did not feel well, not at all. She noticed the longer she sat there, she was becoming so hot, her head started spinning and her heart was racing so rapidly, that she thought that she was about to lose consciousness. It had become so bad that she literally felt like she was going to die. The only thing that she could do was to sit there and pray that God would not let her die, not here and not now. Considering they were there with their friends, she didn't want to make a disturbance or alarm anyone, so she uttered not a word, not even to her husband. She simply placed her head on her husband's shoulder and she sat and waited for the service to be finished.

It felt like those few hours were becoming days. She just wanted to get out of there and get some air, she really thought that this was her time to die. She recalled thinking; as long as she doesn't declare her feelings and thoughts, perhaps it will all go away. Inevitably, she had no alternative, she had to say something, because the service had concluded and now it was time for her to get up and she just couldn't. She explained to her husband what was happening to her, and it terrified him to death. Their friends hastily went to obtain assistance. They were able to locate a nurse. The nurse examined her and discovered that her pulse was racing a mile a minute; and with all the excitement and embarrassment, she began improving slightly.

There were people standing all around her — looking — making space so that she was able to acquire air — all observance was on her. She believes being so self-conscious is what brought her out of that dreadful feeling she experienced. The nurse had inquired of her, if she was pregnant? She didn't believe so, she remembers thinking to herself, if this is how you feel when you are pregnant, she may want to disregard this dream. But deep down inside, they both were yearning that this was the date. She started feeling improvement and they all decided to return to the hotel. The following day, they were set to leave the tranquility of the island and to return back home, to the hustle and bustle of New York. She pleaded with God that the feeling of yesterday would in no way return once more.

They all returned safely home and weeks had gone by. Life had returned to usual. They were all back to the standard of their daily life, moreover, she had relatively forgotten about the horror she had experienced in Jamaica. Roughly a month afterward, she was in bed watching television. It was close to midnight and she got that awful feeling a second time. Her heart started pounding, but this time she realized, she was getting chest pains along with pain down her left arm and she was dizzy and nauseous. She thought she was having a heart attack. She wasn't as fearful as previously, but she knew that something was seriously wrong, but somehow she knew deep down inside, that this was not a heart attack.

She recalls requesting for her husband to make a call to the elder in the church to anoint her. Bear in mind what I said in previous chapters, the Bible says," to call for the elders of the church, and he will anoint you with oil, and the prayer of faith will save the sick." She also asked her husband to telephone their friend, who was a registered nurse and ask if she would come to their home for encouragement. The elder came and anointed her with oil and prayed and also said that God would allow her to understand what her problem was. She remembers feeling notably weak, as though all of her energy had disappeared, but she also remembered that the feeling departed as unexpectedly as it entered and that is the identical thing that transpired the first time. She could not grasp what was happening to her. What was God allowing this time?

The following day came, one that she will at no time forget. It was a cool, autumn day, the sun was shining, but she felt so disheartened and she felt she did not have the energy to even brush her teeth or comb her hair. This was the day they would go to church and with much uncertainty on her part, they ultimately decided to go. She was so weak from fatigue because she did not get considerable sleep the night before, also, she felt so wobbly and she even looked worse than she felt, but something was motivating them to go, so they were determined to be there. She believed that God would take care of her and give her His strength to get prepared and she knew that she would need His power for this current adversity in their life, since this one was touching her health, personally. She recognized some of the decisions her husband had to make and one of them was to trust God for your physical health. This was an act of genuine faith, because to her this was a big decision, on account of, she was scared to death of the unknown and humans fear the unknown.

She knew no matter how turbulent the road is, and whatever the problem or difficulty, He will carry you continuously, if we allow Him and not fight Him every step of the way. This day she was entirely on His shoulders, because since her husband could no longer drive, she had to and she had to fight to keep her thought process on her driving and not center on herself and her problems and fears. They, at last, arrived at church, and all she could do was fall heavily into her chair, feeling so powerless.

There was a friend sitting right behind them and the friend noticed how disturbing she appeared. The friend kept asking what her problem was and if she was all right. She didn't know exactly how to answer, because she did not know what the problem was or what was happening to her. After the service, her friend became so continual, that she demanded to know what was the problem. How do you rationalize, when all she wanted to do is shout to the world, that she feels like she is losing her mind. Not only did she consider she was having heart attacks, moreover, she also felt like her mind was going to explode. Her friend was so gentle and so kind and she took her by the hand and they sat down to converse. She explained to her friend about her heart racing and the dizzy spells and before she could arrange the remainder of her description, her friend took over the discussion and made clear exactly what she had been feeling.

She labeled every symptom and all in all what was happening to her. She was so overjoyed to encounter someone who understood, someone that she could communicate with. Her friend's husband was likewise there to help him understand what was going on and what to look out for, because their friend also suffered with this same feeling/disease. The elder's words kept echoing in her ears, "God will reveal to you just what your problem is," and He did. God worked through this individual to have her know, not only what her problem was, but also, what vitamins to choose to assist her body, because with each attack her body was losing numerous vitamins and minerals and it was essential for them to be replaced. What her problem was, she was suffering from panic/anxiety attacks. Her body had to remain balanced with its vitamins and minerals until God was willing to heal her of this disease. She felt as though she had achieved half the battle by merely knowing what was wrong and also, she was working to keep it under control. There were, yet, going to be bumpy times ahead, because only God knows our future.

She couldn't seem to be able to get liberated from those panic attacks, in fact, they were getting worse. She had lost twenty pounds in just two weeks, because with each attack, her adrenaline would pump so rapidly, it would consume any food that entered her body. That is why it was so important to deposit the vitamins back into her body, because if she didn't, there would be none remaining. She couldn't eat suitably; in fact, she scarcely ate because she felt so nervous, altogether. She felt as though her mind was seizing her body and not in a congenial way. She had become so panicky, that she was developing all types of phobias. Her husband could not leave her alone, because she was terrified of being unaccompanied and also, she feared the nighttime. She could not go out after dark and she rarely went too distant from home in the daylight. She was beginning to be taken hostage by all her fears.

It is so remarkable, how this disease just took over her body and her mind. It is important that we pray for a sound mind because you never really know how vital it is until you feel like you are losing yours. The Bible also says, "that with fear comes torment" (1John:4:18), and that is how she felt. She was continually being tormented of all her fears, she before long became afraid of being afraid. It was as though some gigantic monster was coming to take over her completeness and that she would no longer exist, and she was holding on to the edge of a mountain, praying that someone would rescue her. It is a feeling that can't really be explained, but it is one that you would not want for anyone.

Her husband and their daughter were very helpful; they had to alter their lifestyles, so she was never alone. The three of them just could not comprehend what was happening, nor why this was happening. An additional phobia had entered her life; she had, also, become very claustrophobic. How could she be able to deal with that with all she had to do? She was a mess, but with much prayer from her and her family, she was able to thrust herself into taking charge of her responsibilities. She had to pray that she would not have one of those relapses while outside the home, considering she was the only one in the family that could drive the car.

Her body took awhile before the vitamins would begin working appropriately, since these attacks were removing so much out of her. Unless a person has suffered through this, or observed what she was going through, could they understand anything about this disease. Some thought that she should just snap out of it. She was so frightened because she could not explain exactly how she felt and she felt no one really understood. She also felt that she was to blame for her affliction, because people would want more of her than she was capable of doing and she couldn't give a sane explanation, so she'd just stay away, and remained very close to home. People, who didn't understand, just thought that she was nuts. That is what she really needed to hear.

She was so thankful for her husband, who was by her side every step of the way. There were nights she could not sleep because she would have insomnia. He'd stay awake and just talk to her until she went to sleep. It divulged how a husband and wife were formed to be a helpmate for each other, remember the words in the marriage vows, that all couples take, "for better and for worse" and also, that each partner has to put forth one hundred percent to each other. She never felt so at one with her husband, it felt, as though, they were two halves of a whole, which were joined together at the heart. She saw that her husband was not the only one that needed her, but she really needed him and he was there through every phase of this trial. He needed her, she needed him and they both needed God. She was so afraid that she was relinquishing her sound mind and she couldn't seem to control it.

God was there and gave her the strength to proceed forward and she knew that she had to fully hold fast to Him to get her through the day. She had to take each day, second by second, minute by minute, hour by hour, and then a day, a week, and then a full month. Time became so important to her; it was an accomplishment when she was able to come through the day. She was so thankful for each day that she finished with all her chores, unaltered. God taught her how to liberate herself of certain fears, so that she could care for her family. He showed her, that through sickness, you become humble and it also shows you how to have empathy for others that are having their share of troubles. She had prayed that if anyone was going through this horrible disease, that she could relieve them of their fears. She was astonished when she saw that there were many fellow sufferers. She was able to be there for them so they could have someone to talk to, she was able to encourage them when they had these attacks and let them know that this too will pass. In fact, a good therapy to release your fears and anxieties is to help others; this takes the focus off of the self. God is love, and perfect love casts out fears.

She and her family found themselves opening their home to family and friends, those who just wanted to stop by. Some of their friends had family far away, and so this family became their family and they would all be there for each other. They all needed each other, and she needed her friends, because they helped her through these difficult times, they were there and each of them grew to be an extended family to one another.

She still has the panic attacks, but now she knows how to keep them under control and they don't come as repeatedly as formerly. She still has fears to conquer, but God has been there for her to see her through. Again, this trial that they all went through was a learning experience and yes, God, again, has shown His power and strength and love toward this family. He has not left them nor forsaken them and He promises not to and He won't, because His promises are not counterfeit.

I understand that this book may look as if it is a book of catastrophe, hopelessness and despair, but my emphasis is to inform you that everyone has troubles, some may be worse than others and I'm certain we have all felt let down and discouraged. Sometimes, we don't know what to do or how to get help. We all need help, but our problems may be greater than what we, by ourselves, can manage. We don't have to have a negative perspective of the predicament but, we can have a positive attitude and to notice that we are not alone. We can view the glass as half full and not half empty. We can be assured that whatever the journey, we will never walk alone, if we invite the only One that can help and let Him lead the way.

This was just another battle that they had to encounter and

that only made them unified as a family and the three of them grew stronger by the strength of God. They had to learn how to serve others, and that had to initiate from home. He with no sight and she with her panic attacks learned the word **GIVE**. They could not think of themselves, they knew they needed each other and during these uneasy times that they both needed their daughter and the three needed God. He always will make a way of escape, if we trust Him.

Her husband, also, had to adapt to his anxieties while his vision progressively got worse, knowing that there was a likelihood, that one day, he would be in total darkness. A darkness that we can never imagine. He would forgo his self-confidence and not be able to do what he was in the habit of performing and all this happened at such a young age; and now they had to deal with her fears that came with her panic attacks. You learn how to have mercy and compassion for others and you realize that what you see is not always the way it appears. I can see why God said that He does not look at the outside appearance but at the inside of one's heart. You can always help others, who have a disability or illness, even if it is just in prayer and that is the most important support, because you are taking it to the only One that can help. Remember that nothing is impossible with God, nothing at all and you don't have to ever be ashamed of whatever difficulty you are having. Always treasure this, God knows all things and also, He loves it when we come to Him and that is the reason why He has so many promises for us mere mortals. He knows we make many mistakes and as you will see when reading the Bible, that man has made innumerable blunders from the beginning of time, but He is there to help us out of all our situations. Remember Jesus wants us to cast all our cares on His shoulders, because He says, "His yoke is easy and His burden is light" (Matt. 11:30).

CHAPTER FIVE
How Long?

Do you believe it; we have gone through two decades already, the seventies and the eighties. When you look over these past two decades, you may feel a little discouraged and maybe a bit sorry for this family. That was not the intention of this book, not at all. It is meant to show us all the power, the mercy, the compassion, and the love that our great Father has for us. It is also to show us that we are not alone and that we all have troubles, no matter how big or how small they are. I remember the words to this song which goes, "His eyes are on the sparrow and we know He is watching us." The Bible even tells us how God feeds the birds of the air and then asks us, "are we not of more value than they?" Yes, He is in control of all things BUT He also allows things to happen.

God is not asleep on the job. Sometimes we have to look at ourselves and ask if we may have brought certain problems on ourselves. But always, God is there to listen and help but when we do put our burdens on the shoulders of Christ, we will go right back and pick up those same burdens and put them back on our shoulders, instead of leaving them with Christ. We need to learn how to get rid of the problem, also to leave it and rely on Christ. That is why we all have to go through troubles in order to learn how. We have the choice; to either make the problem easier or harder. God even gives all human beings a choice. Whether we choose the right way or the wrong way, we still have the choice and with the choices we make come consequences, whether they are good or bad.

So here we are, in the decade of the nineties. The beginning of this decade, was one of this couple's proudest moments, when their daughter graduated from high school. This is the year 1990. They were so happy for her. She was no longer their little girl, she was now about to become a woman and getting ready to enter college. Where did all the years go? She always did very well in school; in fact, when she graduated she won several scholarships and awards that helped with the expenses of college. This was it, the day that she would march down the aisle for her graduation ceremony where there stood her principal awaiting to present her and her fellow classmates their diploma. Every family member that could attend did attend. She was so involved in the activities of her high school, that they even mentioned her name during one of the speeches that was given by one of the teachers. She had grown up to be a really nice young lady. Everyone was so proud of her and her accomplishments. After the beautiful ceremony, family and friends went back to this family's home for a barbecue to help celebrate their daughter's happy day.

She had decided that she wanted to go to a local college and study teaching. This made it good for her parents because they were not quite ready to let her go, the reason being, in their eyes she was still their little girl no matter how old she was. It was a little easier for her mother to allow her to spread her wings, but for her father, he was not quite ready. He could not believe that she was growing up so fast and also starting to date. Of course, no man was ever good enough and after much hesitation, he would let her go to have a good time.

Their daughter had so many talents and a lot of drive and she was also able to accomplish whatever she set out to do because she was taught from childhood how to let God lead her life. While in high school, she was on the school newspaper. She enjoyed journalism. She even had a job as an intern for a computer magazine while she was in college. She had her own office and desk and even had some of her articles published.

She also spoke several languages, which later on she taught at a language school while also in college. She had grown and was still growing to becoming a well-rounded person, who someday would have many choices and accomplishments that she was adding to her future. God was truly blessing her. It seemed as if everything she had set out to do, she was able to accomplish. Her parents felt so blessed to have this child in their lives and to be able to each share in the raising of this child, to now adulthood. It was starting to look like her life was being molded into a life of happiness.

We know that we have a God that loves us tremendously and that He does not give us more than you can handle (1Cor.10:13). This verse was about to be tested. It seemed that the past two decades were just a forerunner for what was ahead for this family. When the patriarch Jacob wrestled with God and would not let go until God blessed him, this family did not know that they were going to have to hold on to their Creator for dear life and not let go.

It starts in the year 1993 and the month is April. Their daughter had gone out to meet some of her friends and they had decided to go visiting and when it was time to leave from their destination, their daughter got into her car alone and proceeded to drive home. On the way home, she was in a very bad car accident. She had crashed and her car was wrapped around a pole. She was all right after an event of many miracles. The car was totaled and she was badly injured. Their little girl was unconscious in the car and the fire department had to cut her out of the car because the car was so badly damaged around the pole. The car was in such bad shape, that the people that witnessed the accident just knew she was dead. When they finally got her out of the car, the very next second, the car was engulfed in flames. They saw that she was alive, but during their examination they noticed the way her legs were just dangling and they thought that she was either paralyzed or that her legs were severely broken. Her face was so swollen that those who knew her barely recognized her. They put her on the stretcher and put her into the ambulance and rushed her to the nearest hospital.

Their daughter was in such pain that she thought that she would blackout and the doctors continued sending her for tests to see if she had any internal damage and they just knew that something had to be broken especially her jaw. Her parents, family and friends prayed for God's intervention and guess what, that's right; here came God to the rescue for this family once again. All her tests came back negative, nothing was broken; her swelling went down that night and the pain was gone completely. Even her cuts, which were quite deep, got scabs that very evening and she was able to come home the next day. Thank God no one else was in the car with her. This day was one of the most frightening days because they thought that their child was going to die. But, our Deliverer was right there and delivered them once again.

The next month was May 1993 and this was one of the most horrifying days of her husband's life. This was the day that his mother had died suddenly from a heart attack. She was not sick and had no known heart problems. In fact, he had just spoken to his mother just a few hours before she died. Two months in a row, last month it was their daughter and now his mother. This put them into an emotional, mental and physical turmoil. These twenty plus years were beginning to take its toll. It felt as if their entire world was falling down on them, they felt as if they could not go on, they could not take one extra step. They started to forget all the deliverances and all the promises that God had made. They even questioned, is all of this worth it? They just wanted to die and give up and throw in the towel. They could not see the light at the end of the tunnel anymore and they could not see themselves making it another day.

He had felt like a big part of his life was gone. He wanted so much to have been able to see her just one last time. This was one time he hated being blind and really wanted his sight. They prayed, "why God, why now?" This was his mother; she was so young and never reached the ripe old age of seventy. It felt like a big chunk of his childhood was gone and all he was left with were his memories.

But God gave this family time to sorrow and then He stepped in and gave them an extra boost of His strength. God knew that this was a big loss for them, especially him, because this was his mother, the woman who loved him and cared for him throughout his childhood to adulthood years, but He gave them the strength to keep right on going forward and even let them see the blessings of it all and the main one is that she never had to suffer, she just when peacefully and speedily.

The same year 1993, something else happened to test their faith and trust in God. Three of her closest relatives, who could not have children, became pregnant. They too waited for years, hoping that one day they would have their very own child. That day had come for the three of them and their spouses, all three became pregnant at the same time. She felt like a knife was put into her heart and that it was ripped out of her chest. She felt like her entire insides was about to come out through every opening of her body. She didn't want to be jealous or envious of anyone, she wanted to be happy for them. They too, had waited for years and wanted so much to have a baby and now it was their turn. She didn't wish it were she instead of them, she just wished that she could have made it a foursome. You know that God was testing this family's faith, He wanted to see if they would give up on Him and His promises. It was so hard for them to think of or even remember the promises, because it hurt so bad and the pain clouded their memory. They had even asked themselves, "if God really loved them?" But they knew deep down inside that He did. When you have doubts creeping into your mind, always remember what God has done for you in the past and that will help strengthen you.

They went back to the Bible and saw the story of Hannah.

She too wanted her very own child and also waited a long time for God to keep His promise to her. Hannah's husband's other wife had several children and Hannah was so hurt because she was unable to have not even one child. But Hannah went to God and presented Him with her request and she waited and also, held on to the promise and God finally did bless Hannah with not just one but several children of her own and one of them God had used for His work. She trusted God and He had come through for her.

It helped this family to hold on and continue to wait patiently. They remembered there was nothing that was impossible with God and that He will keep His promise to them. They were really happy for their family members who gave birth to happy and healthy babies. This couple had no envy or jealousy toward the others; just joy and they loved those little ones and was happy to be a part of their lives. Yes, it still hurts at times and she may even question, "why not me too," especially when she sees the biological clock ticking and time is passing and still nothing. But she is thankful for her little girl and their family life and she will continue to wait for God to come forth with His mighty hand and bless her with her own from her body.

They started, once again, to have financial troubles. God was beginning to permit another trial to enter their life, by allowing a substantial amount to be reduced from his disability insurance and also the job his wife had, working from home, had gone bankrupt, which meant that she no longer had a job. As time went on, things in the house needed work and the car needed the essential fixings done. What could happen, did happen. With the missing income, they needed something to fill the void. Debts started accumulating and it felt like God had gone away for awhile. It was such an empty feeling, that they, for the first time, felt all alone and it was not a pleasant feeling. They really started to become afraid. It felt like they were out in an open war zone and you never knew when a bullet or something would hit you and you had no protection, at least that is how you felt.

They again had gone to the Bible searching for answers and they both related to the story of Job. The story shows how God allowed Satan to take away all that Job had, his health and his possessions. Job kept crying out to God and God did not immediately answer, but the story shows how God was there and was always in control, but did not make Himself known to Job until He was ready. This couple felt the same emptiness that Job did. God tells us, like I said previously, that He will never leave us nor forsake us, but there are times that God will have His hands off of the situation to see just what we would do and what we are made of.

Do you remember the promise that He will not leave us? Think about it, if someone leaves, who did the leaving? It must have been us, but like I said there are times that He will have hands off. Job kept right on crying out to God just like this family did, but God will sometimes keep His distance until He is ready. We all can start taking God for granted and think He has to help us when we want and with what we want. Do we stick with God with the bitter and with the sweet? He has to see just what we are made of. We, ourselves, don't have an idea what we are made of.

They tried so hard to think of ways to pay their bills. But how? God had brought them through in the past, so they knew He would bring them through the present, as well as the future. Look at the end of the story of Job, God had restored all that Job had lost and doubled everything. So this couple would continue to wait and trust God and believe His promises and trust He will see them through.

Things started happening one right after the other, this time, once more, it was their daughter. This one would be the trial of all trials; this is the one that was the final straw, the one that would destroy their family.

As was spoken previously, their daughter was going to college locally and she seemed to be doing quite well. She continued to get good grades in her classes and also had a very good job. About three years after her high school graduation, her parents started noticing little changes in her. She seemed to very quiet and they thought that to be strange because she was a very talkative person and very social and loved to have a good time. Things just didn't seem right, nothing that you could really pinpoint. During her last year, she had decided to stay on campus, because she was taking so many classes at various times and that it would be easier for her to live on campus and not have to travel at all different hours. Her parents also agreed, because they wanted her to be somewhere that was safer than traveling at all hours of the night. Their daughter would come home on weekends and spend time with her parents and her friends.

And then one day something happened, the weekend she was suppose to come home, she did not show up. No phone calls, no anything. They had no idea what could have happened. They had called her friends to see if they had seen her, but they hadn't and they hadn't even heard from her. All kinds of things started going through their head, they couldn't imagine where she was or even worse, what could have happened. They decided to go to the police department and file a missing person's report. This could not be happening; they both wished they would just die at that very moment. They were so tired of all these things happening to them, they couldn't imagine how much more they could take. It was as if their entire life had gone up in smoke; their once happy family was gone and they couldn't do a thing about it. They just wanted their daughter back home, "please dear God, not this too."

Their life was materializing into some science fiction movie, one that had a frog that was placed in a pot of cold water. Each day, someone would gradually make the water warmer while the frog stayed in. With the gradual change in the water temperature, the frog never noticed the water was growing hotter, until one day the poor frog boiled to death. That is how they felt, at that instant, like they were boiled to death, without warning. What could have happened, kept going through their heads. They even tried to think positive, but every fear and every tragedy that could have transpired, entered their thoughts.

After what seemed to be the longest five months in history, as if time had just stood still, they had finally heard from their daughter and she seemed to be physically all right. It had seemed that her entire past, from the ages of birth to the age of two, had all come to the surface. Her entire life felt as though it were in question and she felt as if she had been abandoned by her biological mother, and she also felt as if she did not belong anywhere. The night she came home, the three of them talked all night. They had tried to come up with some answers to all the questions and feelings that were stirring up inside of her, but it is really difficult for a person to recognize what another person is going through unless we have been there. The best thing her parents could do was to listen and to show, no matter what, they loved her and that they were there and would not leave her.

Even their daughter could not make sense out of what was happening to her, she had feelings, emotions and fears flying in all different directions, with no right course to follow and her mother could truly relate to that because of what she has been suffering with her panic attacks. Their daughter had no pictures of herself until the age of two, when she came home with them and had no one to tell her about those first two years of her life. All of her anxieties did not hit her until she turned twenty-one and it all just came crashing in, with not one question, she felt, could be answered logically and to her satisfaction. Her parents suggested that she talk to someone, who was neutral, so that she could speak her mind with no embarrassment. Her parents heart broke for her, because this time they knew this problem could not be fixed with just a Band-Aid nor with all the love they had for her. She needed answers that they could not give her.

Her parents noticed that she started to really change. She seemed to have given up on all her desires and wants for the future. She had changed her friends and started socializing with ones that she would not bring home and then their biggest nightmare came to life when she started using drugs. Her parents were no longer able to be there for her the way they use to be, they were losing her to something that was beyond their control. She even dropped out of college in her last year, in fact, in her last semester. It looked like she was now trying to find herself or even, maybe, escape from herself but she was going all in the wrong direction, she was growing out of control and in a very destructive way. Again, only if you have been through the feeling of abandonment by our biological parents, could we fully understand or judge and each of us handles our problems in different ways because we are all individuals. Again, the only One that could help in this situation was God and her parents prayed for Him to help their daughter with whatever problem she may be facing and also to help her to come to terms with it.

Their daughter decided that maybe it was time that she got her own apartment. Her parents thought that maybe this would be good, to give her a chance to try and understand what may be happening. They felt so useless, but knew the only thing they could do was to be there for her whenever she needed them. This couple knew from their experiences with trials, that when they needed moral support from family and friends, most times they just needed to know that you have someone who really cares and is there if you need them. Their daughter thought that maybe moving away, somewhere that was different, with new beginnings, should and could help her. A place where she knew nothing about. A place where she could start all over again, as she was now an adult and she also realized that she needed to start acting like one, so she decided to move to Atlanta, Georgia. While she was there for a short period of time, the move proved to be a good one and she seemed to be really making a positive improvement. She had gotten a good job, one that had good advancements and also one that she seemed to enjoy. She stopped using the drugs and also started realizing how special she was, no matter what her biological parents did and that she had parents and a family that loved her. Their relationship seemed to be back on the road to being "the three of them" again. Her sense of humor was back and her wonderful personality was again starting to peak. It seemed she was coming back to them. She had a beautiful apartment and also bought herself a car. She seemed to be going toward the life that she was destined to have, a great and wonderful one.

And then again, her parents started noticing that they had not heard from her in awhile, days started going into weeks and so on. They thought to themselves, not again, please not again and their fears resurfaced again, because yes, it was again. She was gone! What could have happened? She seemed so happy again, she had a good job, she had all the necessary essentials, but they guessed she must not have had the one essential that she really needed and that was, who she was. They tried so hard to find her, and to no avail. Where could she have gone? They even had a private investigator look for her. It was as if she had vanished from off the face of the earth. She was gone once again! This time it seems that she has chosen not to be found, because it has now been a little more than four years and they still have not heard a word. All the questions they have, with no one to give them any answers, is worse than the death of a child because at least with death, it gives you closure. But this is horrible! It is the unknowing, if she is dead or alive and if she is sick or hurt and there is nothing, nothing at all that they can do but wait. Each and every time the phone would ring and they would answer and if the person would hang up, they'd wonder if it was her. They felt as though they were driving down this long, dark highway that had utterly no exits, it was a path that they could not get away from, they felt lost and they could not find their way back home, ever again.

That same Being that has kept this family together, through all these years, is still doing so. They had to do the hardest thing they ever had to do, and that was, to once again, put this entire situation in the hands of God. This time it was a little harder, because this was their child and they didn't know where she was or how she was, they knew absolutely nothing, except that God knows where she is and also, what she is feeling at this very moment. He knows her heart and her pains. Our past is the key to our future and the key to the future is our present. Pain can start in a person's life right from conception. A child can sense if their biological parent wants them or not. That child can feel and sense the love of a parent. That is why it is very important that we start our parenting skills right from the start because the parents can be the key to a lot of their child's problems. Being a parent is an awesome responsibility; we can not take it likely. Children cannot raise themselves; they must be nurtured and loved right from birth. It is hard for a child to feel love later on when they felt that they were not wanted from the beginning. Thankfully, we have a God that loves us much more than any human could, and they know that He is watching over her and will be there for her, no matter where she is.

They pray that their little girl can one day feel the love that God has for her and that He will bring to her memory the love her parents have for her, always. Their little girl is gone for now. They don't know where she has gone, but they pray that God will unlock the prison doors in her life and give her back her freedom and the map back home and into the arms of her parents, who await everyday for her homecoming.

We all have things in our past, some that are good and some

that are bad, some we want to forget and some we want to remember, but whatever it is, we are all products of it. But we do not have to become victims of our past, no matter how bad it was, because God can see us through any situation. This couple prayed all the time that their little girl will remember what she was taught from childhood and that God is there to help her and loves her, no matter what she has done and also to know, that no matter how bad the situation, He will hold her hand and bring her through; back to where she belongs, to where He wants her to be and also, to be happy.

Life for this couple was a fantasy, one that didn't seem real, not at all but it wasn't the fantasy they imagined before they had their fairy tale wedding. They had dreamed that their life would go on happily ever after, but this life was far from the dreams they had, it is not one that they could have ever imagined for themselves. She sat back and looked over the past twenty-five years and saw all that was gone, in addition to all that was lost. So much they had lost, their finances, he lost his eyesight and most importantly, they had lost their child. But again, let us go back to the story of Job. He had the same losses, his finances, his children and his health. But Job patiently waited for God to do His will and God came through for Job. God's servants say over and over again, that God delivered them from all their troubles, no matter how big or how small the problem was and these two believed that and continued to hold on.

Even their health started becoming affected from all the stress. They would wake up every morning with all types of muscle aches because they were never able to relax, in fact, there were times that they had insomnia and was unable to sleep. Sleep had become their only way of escape because they would be unconscious to their real life horrors and there were times they couldn't even have that. With no sleep and being in

71

constant stress pain, they started becoming depressed more and more and would find it harder to come out of the depression. They would have to push themselves from day to day, just to make it through the day and unto the next day. They started questioning, how much more can a human being take? But God would continue to show this couple that He was with them and that He did not leave them. He was still blessing them with many blessings, and also, they had friends that stuck by them through all their difficulties. Their friends even got together and painted this family's house for them and made it look brand new. So God was blessing them, but still this family wanted to know, how much longer, how much longer did they have to wait before God would deliver them, because physically and emotionally they did not think that they could hold on much longer, they really didn't. They felt as though the rope was about to pop and they would come falling to earth and no one would be there to catch them. They had to hold on tight to each other and not let go, even when they thought they were going to lose their mind. "Dear God, how much longer?" No one ever really knew the sufferings this family had to endure.

Sometimes they wanted to yell from the rooftop, but why complain they thought; they never, ever wanted people to feel sorry for them. There were times their insides felt like they were just being ripped out because of the hurt and pain. They never knew what it meant to have your heart break until these last few years, because they lived with a continual heartbreak. But this family just kept going forward and always with a smile. There were moments when they just wanted to stop living and give up on life, but they couldn't fail God and they didn't want to disappoint Him, but still, "how long?" They continued to believe the promises and said to each other, "they would rather die trusting in God, than living and not trusting in Him." But how much longer did they have to go before it was over, how long? They felt like they had lost the early decades of their lives, their thirties, their forties and now starting their fifties. They never thought it would take so long, "how long dear God, how long?"

But... God knows best...

CHAPTER SIX
Looking Beyond What the Eye Sees

These past five chapters showed you some of what this family had gone through and some of the things they had lost. It had undoubtedly been a struggle at times. What was mentioned previously, there were days this family really thought that they were losing their sanity. They deplored the day they were born and just wished they had never existed but that, also, was beyond their control. They even thought, at times, that maybe they were born just to be taunted through their adult married life. They wished that they had someone, just one person that could understand or listen without being judgmental, but there seemed to be no one. God seemed to remove that type of person from their midst. The longer this couple went through these trials, they just continued to grow closer toward each other. As the days, months and years passed by, they were becoming inseparable. They were one, as God intended for all husbands and wives to be and they thanked God everyday for each other and for Him.

As you know, life continues to go on as usual, no matter what problems we may be having. As people continued to go about their everyday lives, this couple would feel more and more isolated living in this world. God gave them the strength to continue with their everyday life and people never really realized just what or how this couple was really suffering. They always had that big smile and they continued to entertain at their home with lots of friends and family. They never gave others the impression of their sadness, not unless you looked beyond what the eye saw. This couple even started to feel ashamed of their life, because when they saw how others were succeeding, their life just seemed to stand still as if it didn't move and if it did move, it would move only backwards. But God saw differently. He was teaching them, that when life throws you lemons you learn to make lemonade.

This couple still never once regretted the decisions that they made, even though they felt miserable at times. They had to learn to take the focus off themselves and to put the focus on others, because when you do so you forget about what you are going through. There were some steps that they found helpful in removing the focus off of themselves and learning to care for others. Step number one is *love*. Let's go over the definition of love in order to understand how powerful this word really means. Love can be a fond or tender feeling or a strong or passionate feeling.

In order to refocus our priorities and to take our minds off of our troubles, we have to learn to love each other, but in order to love others, we have to learn to love ourselves. That does not mean that we are to be conceited and think that the world revolves around us. It means that we have to care about ourselves and how we live our lives. We have to have respect for ourselves, in order to have respect for others. To love yourself!

This made them think of their little girl and when she was born and first entered this world and being a newborn, not knowing anything and having to depend on others to take care of her, so that she could immediately have the feeling of safety and love. But she was never able to feel that love and that safety for the first two years of her early childhood. Those two years of her life, she was in foster care and was shuffled from house to house. Since she never felt that love and that safety that most infants experience, she did not know how to feel it within herself and so in turn, she did not know how to really love or trust anyone, fully. She found it hard to trust the love that her parents were giving her or even accept it because she did not feel it for herself from the foundation of her early life, she was not taught how to love herself.

Living on this planet earth, we can look around and see what to do and what not to do and learn from it. We can see how other people do or say things that may be hurtful to others and we can learn not to do the same. You see, we can learn from each other. We can throw away the bad and keep the good. Since this couple had gone through so much during these many years, they have seen and heard a lot of what people have said to them. Some positive and some negative. Sometimes people will speak before they would think, or they will do or say things that they thought to be very helpful but it may have only made the situation worse.

Always remember this key; do not give unwanted advice. Each person is different. Marriage teaches you that each spouse is different and that is one of the hardest things to get use to and learn that we all do things differently. Even when we think in our hearts that if the person does it your way it will help and you may be right, but remember, only if they ask you, give the advice and respect their decision. Sometimes a person just may need you to listen and that's all and you can help by praying for them. This is why we have two ears and only one mouth, to listen and not always speak. Our tongues can cut real deep. Love is suppose to be unconditional, which means, no matter what a person may do or say, we are still suppose to love him or her.

Look at the story of Job, whom we spoke about before, the reason being, this man had been through so much. Well anyway, Job really was suffering and he had his three friends there with him and in their mind they were there to comfort Job. Did they comfort Job? Did they encourage Job? Did they dry Job's tears when he cried to them? No, they just criticized

Job and pointed out what they thought were Job's faults. They made Job's situation worse and that was not their intention, they thought they were helping. Was God pleased? Look at the end of Job's book and you will see the answer is NO.. You see our mouth and our actions can get us in a world of trouble. Love is caring for the welfare of someone, no matter who they are. When we point our finger at someone, we point with one and we have three coming back at us. We must learn to have empathy for others, cry when they cry and laugh when they laugh. Learn to accept the decisions one makes, because first of all, you don't know how they got to the decision and most times, you don't know all the circumstances.

I know for this couple, they both had to make decisions that suited both of them with their disabilities, he with his lack of eyesight and she with her panic attacks and phobias. People thought they should go out and enjoy life. "Go here and go there, do this and do that." Everyone had their opinions, but guess what, for this couple, some places would be more like a nightmare to them then a good time. People thought they were doing the right thing by continuing with their opinions, but guess what would happen, most times this couple would suffer guilt and then depression because they wanted to please others instead of what was best for them. The majority of times, they wanted to do what others wanted them to do, but sometimes they just couldn't. You see, this is why we have to look beyond what the eye could see, because if people did, they would make their suggestion and then, just drop it. Sometimes our love can become suffocating to a person. You can not mold a person to be or act the way you want them to be nor think them to be crazy because they will not let you mold them into your ideal person. Only God molds, He is the Potter and we are the clay. So that means, that we are to keep our molding techniques only to store bought clay. We must learn to do unto others as you would have them do unto you, and if we can remember this, then it will help us in being helpful to others.

Now, the next definition about love that we need to do and this one is a big one, we are to love our enemies... Love our enemies, how do we do that? No matter what anyone may do to us, no matter what, we are to love him or her. Again, this family came across some people that would be considered their enemies, but they saw the best way to help and that is to pray for them and when they did this, they did not have the anger or resentment toward that person anymore. We are human beings and have said some hurtful words or have made some hurtful actions to someone in our lives, one way or another, sometimes unintentionally and sometimes intentionally. We want to be forgiven when we cause harm to someone and that is why we must forgive others. This is why we have to pray for the individual or individuals. Look at King David when Saul was after him, what did he do, he put the situation in God's hands. When someone lashes out at us, we want to lash back at them. Vengeance is not ours, we can not take things into our own hands. Hating someone can lead to murder and we know that is wrong. We can be angry, but don't let it lead to hate and also don't let the sun go down on our anger because it will brew inside of us until we wish only harm to that person. There may be times that we have to stay away from an individual because we may not get along with them and that is all right, but be careful and not let it lead to hatred.

The next thing we can do that can cause distress to someone and that is to spread rumors about that person. We all like to gossip because it makes us look good, it inflates our egos and that shows that we lack confidence in ourselves, so in turn we deflate others. We abase others to esteem ourselves. In reality, it is done for evil and not for good, also, it is done to damage someone's reputation, their character or just to be contemptible. Indeed if the story is correct, for what ever reason we may do it, it can only lead to some type of damage. The person who gossips has nothing else to do but to get into other people's lives. Edify each other. Love looks for the good in an individual and does not rip them apart. Remember the old saying, "if you don't have anything good to say about a person, than don't say it."

The next example of love is the love of a husband and a wife. This symbol of love is different than you would have for an acquaintance or a friend or even a family member. This form of love is a powerful, passionate love for each other. This type of love joins you together and both are to become one. The husband is to leave his father and his mother and cling to his wife and the two are to become one. This is why from time to time, you will be talking to your spouse and the other one is able to finish your sentence or you both may share the very same thought at the very same time. When one hurts, so does the other. You are to be there for each other, no matter what. Remember the words to the wedding vows, the vows that you made to each other, "for better or for worse, for richer or for poorer, in sickness and in health, until death do you part." Those are the promises that married couples made to each other and unfortunately, people no longer seem to take those promises thoughtfully.

In a marriage, we all know, there is more than one person, there are two and someone has to lead, to be the one to take charge. Husbands were made to be the one in control. They are their wife's "knight in shining armor", her Prince Charming. He is the one who protects her from all the hurtful humanity that is out there and he is the one who supports her and makes sure she is content. She is his queen. She is to be treated like royalty. Now, I know that sounds like one of those fairy tale books like the way this book was initiated, but in real life, husbands are to love their wives as they do their own bodies and we know everyone takes care of their own bodies. We nourish our bodies, we cherish our bodies and we don't want anyone to harm our bodies.

A husband is to care for his wife and that does not mean to suffocate her or take away her independence. It means to watch out for her but not going to extremes. Husbands are not to be stern toward their wives and think because they are the "king of their castle", that their wife is their unassuming servant and must do what he says, no matter what or he may give her a pop upside the head and drag her by her hair, caveman style. With that attitude, it will make it terribly hard for a woman to do her part and that is to submit to her husband. It would be very difficult for a woman to submit to a husband, who is literally killing her with love.

His wife is his help-mate, the one who stands by his side, encourages him and the one who builds him up and not tears him down. Remember; behind every successful man is a good woman. Now, I know when I say that a woman is to submit to her husband, some may take this word submit in the wrong way. I am not saying that she is to become his doormat. That is not true. His wife plays an important role. She is the one who runs the house. She is the one that keeps things flowing smoothly. If you look at a housewife, as she goes about her daily chores, observe and watch her at work. Consider how she was created.

She is far from being a fragile and weak individual, in fact; she is a powerful and capable individual. Her day begins with her rising early in the morning and prepares a hearty breakfast for her husband and makes sure he is well fed and then sends him off to work and then she makes sure her children are dressed with proper attire, according to the weather, and fed and sends them off to school. After the house is empty and she is alone, she will wash the dishes, make the beds and clean the house and in between that she is doing laundry. Also, the minutes she has to spare, she is out doing her grocery shopping and takes care of whatever her husband has asked her to do for him and then she comes home just in time to pick up the kids from school and help them with homework and also fix dinner. After dinner, she cleans up and sits down for awhile to spend time with her family and then she prepares the kids for bed and then finally after a long day, she and her husband are alone and then it is time for sleep. Now does this sound like a day of a weak, fragile woman? No! She is a strong creation. She does this for seven days a week, with no days off. But that is all right, because when she has a husband that loves his wife the way he is suppose to, her husband will become her help-mate and will chip in and help when he is able to. That is what love is all about.

Being married teaches you to share and care about others, aside from ourselves, and to give to each other where we may be required. All things worked together in agreement, because this couple, through their many trials, has had to come to the assistance of each other when the other one was unable to accomplish their work, no matter what difficulty they were having, they took their eye off of themselves and put it on their mate. This is the love of a husband and wife, that strong and passionate love, and then, in turn, the two would extend the true meaning of love to their children. It is a circle, what goes around comes around. With families having their faults and all, it helps you to recognize that others have weaknesses and once you realize that, then you are capable to love others. You become less selfish and you are able to take your mind off of your problems and discover the world in a whole different light. You can be there for others by just being an example. It takes two to start trouble and if you don't participate, the other has to stop because they most likely won't talk to themselves. To sum up what love is, it suffers long, is kind, does not envy, is not arrogant, bears all things, believes all things, hopes all things and endures all things; no matter what difficulty there is, love conquers all!

It is now time to progress on to the second step and that is *joy*. The definition of joy is a glad feeling; a glad behavior; happiness. This couple found that if you have love for your fellow man, joy would automatically follow. I won't say that this couple was always able to represent a sense of joy, but they realized that they had an inner feeling of joy. They had to put joy into their lives by learning to have a joyful attitude. Like I said beforehand, they seemed to always have a smile, they were always pleasant and they enjoyed being around people. People don't always want to be near a person who complains all the time and always seems to talk about themselves and who may carry about a dark cloud over their heads.

A person who expresses joy walks into a room and exhilaration will fill the air and not gloom and blues. This may not be an easy task to accomplish, especially when we are feeling miserable; but a smile, at times, will brighten a day. We acquire a goal, something that we may want to achieve, something that you are convinced in and then concentrate on that and do not give up until you have succeeded. We should think positive and encourage others to do so also. If you are constantly thinking negative and anticipate the world is about to cave in on your head, how can you have a sense of joy? No one can experience joy if they are constantly thinking disaster. There are so many positives in the creation, look around you. You can find joy in just watching this small insect called the ant. See how hard they work and prepare from one season to the next, watch how they fight against each colony and protect what belongs to them. Observe the strength in this little creature. Suppose he went about thinking negative all the time and then nothing would ever get done. The ant is a survivor.

Most types or feelings of joy is only temporary, for instance, when you are preparing to go away on a vacation, or watching a good baseball game or movie, or buying new clothes, or just eating a big bowl of ice cream. You waited months for the event to finally come, you may have even spent lots of money for the occasion and then the event has come and gone and then after it is over, so is your joy. This is the type of joy that most of us experience and that is why it is so hard for us to keep it, because it does not last. Some of us try so hard to experience a lasting joy, that we will spend so much money, using our credit cards on who knows what and then our joy leaves, almost immediately when we get the bill and we can't pay it because we don't have the cash money. Where is the joy? Did we find it? This is why this family had to locate a permanent joy, one that would continue, one that would not cease and one that could extend to others.

The one thing that this couple worked very hard to make permanent and that was the joy in their marriage. They both had to search themselves to find out just what would give them the most joy. They had lost so much! Their finances, his eyesight and their child were gone. How could they acquire a permanent joy through all their sorrows? Yes, they still wanted all their prayers answered with deliverances. They still hungered for that each and everyday. They searched each day to discover that lasting joy, that would make them positively happy and the discovery was, that they are to never give up. They started this journey twenty-nine years ago, their path took them down some exceptionally rough roads but they were never alone, not once. These trials were similar to the two of them climbing the highest mountain and with each step they got higher and the task grew harder but they were determined not to give up but to keep right on going forward. Suppose they did decide to give up and then they detected they only had three more steps to take in order to get to the top. Would that have brought them joy or failure? We all have journeys in our lives and if we keep going forward toward our goal and we never give up, once we obtain that goal, I think that would be the ultimate joy because we knew that we never gave up and that we finally reached it with God holding our hand and standing there cheering us on. So right now, this couple is taking baby steps in obtaining that everlasting joy, the one that they keep right on climbing toward each and every day and with God's help; they will make it to the top.

On to the third step and that step is called *peace*. The definition of peace is freedom from strife of any kind; public quiet; freedom from war. Again, when you follow the steps of love and joy, you will have peace entering your life. We should all strive to live at peace with one another, but first you have to have peace within yourself. You may be walking down the street, minding your own business and see a person that has a frown on their face, in fact, you notice this person seems to have had a bad day and their demeanor appears that if someone says the wrong word, an argument could erupt. Do you know that a frown uses more muscles in the face than a smile does? Peace has to start within and then it will extend to your family, home and then others.

We have all known someone who we may not particularly care for and then one day, between you and this person, a problem may arise. We don't race around and try to pick a fight with that person or an argument, we have to be the bigger person and try and solve the problem peacefully. You go to that person with an attitude of gentleness and that will turn away the anger. We can not make a wise decision, if we are angry. It takes two to have a fight, not unless the person is shadow boxing and if that is the case, there is no harm done. Remember that we have to learn to love our enemies.

There are enough wars going on in this world and peace can only start with an individual. Even our children are being programmed to learn anger from an early age. Look at the games, the cartoons and the prime time television shows, all geared toward anger, hatred and murder. It is up to the parents to start bringing peace into their homes so that the anger will cease. We should let peace rule in our hearts and not anger. We should all try and lead a peaceful life, not by causing animosity but tranquility. We are someone's neighbor and remember, the noise that comes from your home can and will affect the person next to you. Some may think that they are living in the world all by themselves, but if we look around, we will see that we are not alone and we should want to bring peace to our neighbor because we are to have that love toward each other. It has to start on our grounds, which is our home. When people come to our homes, let them find the peace that is not in this world today. Doesn't it feel good, when you are at someone's house and everyone is sitting around talking nicely, no cursing, no loud talk, no gossiping and no attacking each other, instead it is a conversation that is uplifting and with laughter and everyone is just feeling relaxed and enjoying each others company and free from any tension and everyone is just having a wonderful time. Isn't that how you want people to feel at your home? We all do.

Life is too short for us to walk around with a chip on our shoulders. If a person makes you angry, go to the person and tell him what you have against him, in a loving and peaceful way. You don't have to go to him with the attitude of "I know I'm right", even if you are, because that person will automatically become defensive and then you know what will happen, an argument will start or even worse a fist fight and what will that solve, nothing at all but maybe some bruises or even broken bones or through no premeditation, death. How many deaths are caused by anger? Think about it, which is better, anger or peace? Bear in mind, when a person's ways are pleasing the Lord, He will make even their enemies at peace with them (Prov. 16:7).

That was also added to the many other teachings that this family had to learn. With all their tribulations, there were times their tempers were flared and there were things that they had to learn and that was to keep it under control because they may say something to someone that could cause serious distress that could never be taken back. Peace had to rule their household in order to make their troubles seem bearable. They would not have been able to control their circumstances if they lived a life of chaos and confusion.

If you have problems bringing peace into your life, we continually have the one, true Peacemaker of all and He will show you how to have peace and how to give up the anger. Blessed are the peacemakers, for they shall be called sons of God (Matt. 5:9). Let peace reign in our hearts, it will make life a little less stressful and you will be surprised what can be accomplished.

Now on to step number four, *long-suffering*. Let's analyze the definition of this word long-suffering, it is enduring trouble, pain, or injury long and patiently. Now this is a word that does make us cringe somewhat, a word that may make us slightly apprehensive, "to suffer long and patiently." This is a word that, too me, is one of the most difficult, because at times, we humans are not patient individuals and want things yesterday and as you can notice, this couple is still waiting, how many years now, for their deliverances. This word long-suffering is positively a test of character and it is also a character builder because waiting patiently doesn't come with a timetable and it is not on our time.

When this family decided that they wanted to put their whole trust in God, in the very beginning it wasn't that difficult, but with each additional trial, things became worse and then started getting harder and then finally everything started snowballing out of control, their control. The trials were not being taken away, but more were being added. When they first got married and decided to wait for God to bless them with a child, that was difficult inwardly, but they were still able to function with their everyday lives and then while they were still waiting, her husband detected that he had glaucoma, but he still had perfect eyesight, so that was not so critical because he was still able to work, but when he lost his sight entirely, his finances became affected and then their life just kept getting progressively worse; their daughter had disappeared and their finances worsened, family members became pregnant and still their was no baby from their body. After twenty-nine years of waiting, they had to discover what long-suffering meant and if they didn't find out and decided to give up, they would have given up on God and His promises.

Who was their Teacher? God... Look at how He has to suffer long, observing us folks down here on earth doing whatever we believe we can do. He has much patience when it refers to us and He wants us to learn how to have patience when it refers Him. If we put our faith and trust in Him, how can we demand Him to answer us when we say He should and then we grow impatient with every waking hour? How would we learn? It is a difficult lesson to learn and that is why He gives us steps in which we are tried. Bear in mind, He doesn't put on us more than what we can handle. So if we have numerous troubles, He must think that we can handle them or else we would not have them, because God does not make mistakes. When God tests our faith, it produces patience (James 1:3).

As we proceed to study on how to become patient with God, we must also exercise and accomplish how to develop patience with one another. This is why love is so important to acquire, because if we don't have love for our fellow man, how will we become patient with them. Living in a world with billions of people, I'm sure we will come across someone, who may do something that is unacceptable to us and we being perfect, will NOT allow that. When it is stated like that, are we able to see how important it is to be patient with one another and accept one's shortcomings? Not one person is alike, we are all made differently, with our own unique distinctiveness and that is also for identical twins. No two people are alike. The way one person may do something, may not be the same way we do it, but maybe we can learn from each other and together be able to find a better way.

It's comical, when we have children we teach them to play nicely with one another, to share their toys, not to argue and not to hit, but to be patient with each other. But when we become adults, we forget our upbringing and we don't play nicely with people that don't do things the way we want them to. We don't share if we don't like you and yes, we will argue with a person that has a different opinion and don't make us really mad because we may even hit you. Who is the grown one? Now, where is our patience? Doesn't it look really offensive, when you see an adult standing in the middle of a store or street or even at home, ranting and raving over whatever? It is the behavior of a child, except you are the adult and here you are having a temper tantrum over something and most times the circumstances are senseless, instead of you just walking away. Does that set a good example to our children? Do we see why God has to test us?

There may be a time when we have to turn the other cheek. God wants us to be patient with all men, to obtain that quality of patience. Again, let's go back to Job. All the anguish he went through, he was patient with his three friends that did nothing but point out all his faults and also, he patiently waited for God to deliver him. Only blessings can come from practicing being patient, because when we lose our control and our patience, our blood pressure goes up and our heart races and at times, we can go into a rage. It can only harm us, if we lose restraint.

Remember the meaning of this word long-suffering, it is a person that endures trouble, pain, or injury, long and patiently. We all treasure things that we have to wait a long time for. Recall something you desired as a child. You told your parents and they told you that you would get it, but they didn't tell you when. You wait and you wait and still nothing. You question to yourself, if your parents lied to you and will they keep their promise they made to you. But you still wait patiently and then one day your parents decide this is the day they will give you what you requested, because they knew that after the wait you would really value it and hold it dear to your heart. The long anticipated day ultimately comes and they kept their promise to you and you received your request. The happiness your heart must have felt, to number one, see your heart's desire being fulfilled and also, they kept their promise. Believe it or not, we all can have that pleasure of that long awaited bliss, if we hold on and wait patiently, whatever the difficulty. If you suffer long, you will win, if you prevail to the end.

Step number five is *kindness*. The definition of this word is, doing good rather than doing harm; friendly; sympathetic; humane. As you notice, each step always goes back to the word love. If you don't have love for one another, how can you be kind to one another? There are so many ways that you can be kind to someone. This word can be practiced everyday of our lives and is unquestionably a positive form of character. It is a type of giving, which means our focus is off one's self and it is not a type of getting because that shows our focus on one's self.

As we look at the definition, we can look at the meaning of doing good rather than doing harm. It is so much easier for us to do good to someone who likes us, but what about doing good to someone that may not like us. Do we do harm to them? Thankfully, this couple was able to observe the example of their family and friends and how they had come to this couples aid when they needed them and how they were treated. They remembered a time when it had snowed so deep, from a blizzard, the night before and it was going to be difficult for him to shovel this much snow with no eyesight and it was too abundant for her to do all alone, but they had no choice but to proceed outside to start shoveling and before their shovel could touch the snow, they heard a noise of a car behind them and as they turned around they saw some of their friends right there ready, willing and able to help. This couple never asked, they just came because they knew that their help was needed. Was this not an appearance of kindness? Another incident, a special occasion or their anniversary would take place and he, being blind, had no means to get to the store to go shopping for a card or a gift for her, but without fail and again not asking, here to the rescue, another friend, who would keep in mind these special occasions and would come to the house and take him shopping and they would go out and buy her gift for every occasion. Was this too, not an appearance of kindness?

Also, what was spoken about earlier, about this couples house which needed to be painted and a group of their friends got together and painted their home. The list could go on and on, but do you see what I am saying? These people looked beyond. There may be times that you can't do physical labor for someone who may be in want, but what about a phone call, just to let them know that you are thinking of them and don't just call to dump your problems into their lap but listen to what they may have to say. There are many widows in this world that live alone and we all can think of one, maybe they are lonely and even if they are not, they may want someone to talk and share some occurrence in their life and your one phone call may have made their day.

Now, let's go to the next definition, friendly. A smile is just a frown turned upside down. Life, itself, is filled with so many stresses, but do we have to show it on our face or in our attitude? I know we are to share, but can't we keep to ourselves our bad days or bad attitudes. Sometimes when we leave our homes and we enter a world of different people with different situations and attitudes and from time to time, someone can make or break our day. Here is an illustration... you go to the grocery store and after you shop, you go to the checkout counter so that the cashier can ring up your items. As you are putting your items on the belt, you notice that the cashier seems to have had a bad day and they are determined to try to ruin yours. Their attitude is so grouchy, they are barely looking at you and as they are ringing up your groceries, they just fling your items from one side of the belt to the other and then finally, they start bagging your belongings with the eggs on the bottom and then they gaze at you with a look, as if to say, "you better not say a word" and then, they yank your money from your hands and at last, they send you on your way with no smile or even a thank you. How does that make you feel? Does that perhaps take away your cheerful attitude or put you into the mood similar to the cashier?

Now let's compare the reverse side of this illustration. You go to the grocery store and after you finish shopping you go to the checkout counter. As you are placing your items on the belt, you notice the cashier, whose facial expression is of delight, so much so, that she even says, "good morning" with a smile, as she rings up your groceries, she carefully places your items from one side of the belt to the other, after she finished bagging your items with care, she gently takes your money and sends you on your way, with a smile and says "have a good day." Even if you are not in a courteous mood, the odds are, after you leave that grocery store with the cashier that had a pleasant attitude, you might exhibit a better mood. Do you see what I mean? A little smile can go a long way. No one wants to be near a grump, except maybe another grump. Being neighborly can simply bring joy to someone else's life. You can hold the door for someone in back of you, even if you have had the door slammed in your face by someone else. People learn from example.

The subsequent meaning of kindness is being sympathetic. In the event you see a person hurting in someway, physically, mentally, or emotionally, enable them moral support. Be positive, listen and don't be judgmental.

Last but not least of the definition is, being humane. Humane is not being cruel or brutal. There are numerous people being cruel to one another, physically and as well as emotionally. You may not intend to be mean to an individual the majority of times, but there are times we hurt others with our big mouths. It may not be so much what we say, but how we say it. There is nothing worse but to hear a spouse speak to the other in such a bitter way. That can be as bad as physical abuse. Words can cut deep like a knife. Let's observe our anger and be careful what we say or how we say it and don't let our anger brew up inside of us and then explode. We can even be humane to God's creatures. You notice several people who own an animal and abuse them. Keep in mind, they have feelings also, and they, as well, belong to God. King David was a shepherd before he became king and he, at times, would have to fight away animals to protect his sheep. That is how much he loved God's creatures, especially the ones he was accountable for.

This couple learned the meaning of kindness because of the many ways kindness was shown to them by family and friends. They learned by the example of others. They knew they had to learn to be kind to each other and to care about the other's feelings because they spent the majority of their time together and they knew they wanted to live in harmony and peace with each other. If each person in the world took time to be kind to one another starting in the home, it would expand throughout the world and it can be an improved place in which to live.

Follow the greatest example of all, the example of Jesus Christ and how He was so good, so friendly, so sympathetic and so humane to others. No matter what they did, or how they acted, He was always so kind and even at the cruelest time in His life, when they killed Him. Look at His last words, see how kind He was to mankind when He said, "Father, forgive them, for they know not what they do" (Luke 23:34). Live by those words and that will help us all to be kind and to forgive each other, because some of us may know not what we do.

As we move along to step number six, which is *goodness*. The definition of this word goodness is, behaving well; one that does what is right; honorable and devout. As you can see by these steps and their definitions, they are all linked together one way or another. We all value the friendship of a person that we can trust. An individual that you can confide your deepest and darkest secrets to and know that person will restrain from telling anyone. A person's word means everything, you can trust on what they say, their yes is yes and their no is no. Their word is true. We are to be honest with each other and not be considered a liar. How can you trust a liar, their word means nothing. God hates liars (Prov. 6:16-19). That is why, when we make a promise to someone, we must keep it. We have to be a person of our word. We must watch what we say and try not to make promises to each other because one day we may feel one way and then the next day we may feel another way, so don't make promises that we can't keep. This couple had to learn this the hard way, because they would make promises to be somewhere and at times, her husband would suffer some discomfort with his eyes and they would have to back out and also, with her panic attacks, one day she'd feel great and then the next day, she felt as though she couldn't make it out the door. So they learned to say to others, "they would try."

We humans appreciate a person that sets goals for themselves and then goes after them until they are accomplished, they practice what they preach. For this couple, people just knew that when the going got tough, they would run for the hills with their tails between their legs. When the going gets tough, we have to look to God, so that the tough can get going. We have to fully have no doubt in the decisions we make. There is nothing worse than seeing someone stopping in the middle of their goal and then giving up. Suppose God gave up on us and at times He has reason to, but with His goodness He provides our every need and looks for nothing in return. We, too, can do good to others in many different ways. Clothe the poor. I'm sure some of us have a house full of old clothing that is just sitting there collecting dust. Why not pack them away neatly and give them to a group that distributes to those in need. Be there for the fatherless. Look around and see all the children about with only one parent in their lives. Be an example, make yourself accessible to them and when they may have a problem or just need a man to throw a baseball or a woman to just brush their hair, you are there to care for their needs. Jesus Christ loved the children. He even said that we have to have the attitude of a child toward Him (Matt. 18:4). A little child looks to their parents for total dependence and that is the way we are to look to Him, for our dependence. Take care of the widows. Like I said previously, call them and see how they are feeling. Maybe they need to go grocery shopping, make yourself serviceable to them. There are so many ways we can help. We can help those less fortunate and not expect to be praised for our good deeds, do it in secret, and don't blow your own horn. It is better to give than to receive.

There are good deeds we can find to do to help others. Look at the news, everyday it is full of so many corrupt deeds. This family was determined they would make a difference, but it had to start within. Start to develop goodness within yourself and eventually it will spread to others and others may just follow your example.

The seventh step is *faithfulness*. The definition is, one who is worthy of trust; doing one's duty; keeping one's promise; loyal. Each step is very similar in meaning and it is a character that we are trying to build in order to become a complete individual. One that will make us strong individuals, one that will help us throughout all types of troubles, one that shows that we are not alone and that we are here to help others.

Through this couple's trials, God took them through various steps or classes. They started taking baby steps and advancing to adult steps, but God showed them who He is and how they can grow to depend solely on Him, no matter how difficult the situation and also that He was there to cheer them on to victory. But there were lessons they still had to learn; they had to get to know who He was. Even though they still have their trials and He has not yet delivered them, He can still be trusted. How? They are still hopeful, depending on Him, looking to Him, knowing that He is not just someone of some invisible power, but one that you can feel the love and comfort He has to give. He has shown them various miracles and He is still teaching them to trust Him, no matter what. He is also one who keep's His promises. Like I said before, God hates liars and what would it look like if He were one. He has a Book full of promises, promises He will not break, but there are things we have to do, things that we have to learn before His mighty hand will come through for us. His Word is a book of things that He wants from us, but we humans have a tendency to do what we want to do and we can't have it both ways. He keeps His promises to us; do we keep our promises to Him? And yes, God is loyal to us. He is a true and a faithful Friend to us. He loves us, no matter what. He is our Counselor, He is our Deliverer and He is our Healer. He is all things to us, but we have to let Him into our lives. You see, He teaches us, so then we, in turn, can help others.

Are we worthy of trust? When we become man and wife, we take a vow to each other and that is to be faithful to each other. We are to be there for each other and not go outside the marriage for other partners. Can our mate solely depend on us? Do we forgive each other and not hold faults over each other's head for the rest of their lives? Are we truthful? Are we sneaky? When we ask ourselves these questions, "are we the type of person we would trust?" We must examine ourselves and see the person we are. Remember; love ourselves, so we can love others. Be the best person we can be, so we can bring enjoyment to others. Do we do our duty? Do we take care of the things we are suppose to? We have ourselves, our homes and our jobs to care for. Some of us have spouses and children. It must start at home. We are to do things to the best of our abilities. Don't be lazy; always want to be a doer and not a taker. I spoke about this before, about keeping our promises.

We want to be a person of our word. And we also want to be loyal, one that brings joy to someone else. If you would observe the demeanor of a dog, watch and see how loyal he is to his owner. No matter how the owner may treat him, he is always so happy to see his master. His love and loyalty is unconditional. That is what we are to be toward others. Our love and loyalty has to be unconditional because people will always make us angry and if that person is in trouble, what are you going to do, shut the door in his or her face? I hope not, I hope you will be there for that person and not bring up the past but just accept the present. Forget the past; move on to the future. Forgive each other's faults, no matter how many times we are faulted.

God is so faithful to us all, no matter what our situation and wouldn't it be great if He could say to each of us, "well done My good and faithful servant." Let us not give up on God or each other. Strive to be that good and faithful servant.

The eighth step in this learning experience is *meekness*. The definition is, not easily angered; mild; patient; gentle. As was continuously referred to, this couple had to learn how not to be easily angered. First of all, because of the decisions they had made, which was not what you would call "conventional", people, most times, could not understand why this couple would select the method they chose and so, in turn, people would state that the problems they were having was brought about only by them. Once in a while, they were made to believe that they were the ones to blame because they thought that they were not living up to others expectations of them. They were made to feel like failures and at times, this couple felt like just bursting with anger at those that made them feel this way and they felt as though they had to justify themselves. But they had to learn to put themselves in other peoples shoes and realize that if the roles were reversed they may have done or said the same exact thing. The majority of times, people did or said things because of fear and not to be cruel. They feared that this couple was making these decisions that just did not make any sense. So once you recognize that people are entitled to their opinions, you will also see that you will not allow them to make you so angry and you can discover how to overlook their opinions that may be meant to strike out at you.

The next part of the definition is mild. That is to be tender to one another not rough. You know how a new mother is with her newborn baby; she is so tender and gentle to her infant. Why can't we be that way to others? Treat each other with tender loving care, realizing that we all have genuine feelings. Also, be pleasant and not harsh with one another. Some people behave with others, like a bull in a store full of china, they just stampede over each other, not caring who they strike or wound in the process. Learn to be sensitive to others with their feelings, needs and wants. This is why family is so important, because it teaches us not to get irritated with each other or bent out of shape and also, we learn from our trials. A meek person is also a person that is teachable, one that is not easily angered; he will listen when spoken to. We learn by listening and not always speaking. You can't communicate with a hot-tempered person and most times, you don't want to. A hot-tempered person will give the opinion that they know it all and that you can't teach them anything. How can God deal with someone like that? We should always want to learn. Life itself is a learning experience. Look at all the life discoveries this family has been through.

Being meek does not mean being weak. The bible says that Moses was one of the meekest of men (Num. 12:3). Look at the responsibilities he had and the amount of people he had to lead. They were not what you would claim to be the easiest people; they were demanding, they scarcely did what they were told and they were always blaming Moses, but he was very patient with them and even had to plead with God for them because he cared and loved them. We have to learn how to live with one another and how to get along.

Now to the concluding step, last but not least, is *self-control*. The definition of this word is, control of one's actions or feelings. We must all strive to be in control of our actions. I believe that I have shown throughout this book, that having control of our actions is so essential. We should put ourselves in the place of God, for just one moment, during the times that He is watching us and seeing how we act; He indeed has total control because He has not yet wiped us off the face of the earth. We have made many mistakes in our lives, to Him and to others and with Him having self-control, He is patient with us. You can investigate the bible and see the actions of others and you will be able to see His love, compassion and mercy that He has toward humanity. We learn by reading the bible and it will teach us how to treat others. Again, we will continuously run across individuals that will make us angry and we must have control of our actions.

This word does not only apply to anger management, but it could be any weakness we may have. It could be drinking, it could be eating, it could be shopping, it could be watching television, it could be a number of things, any weaknesses we may have, it all has to be done in moderation, and we have to have self-control. There may be a time when a spouse may work numerous extended hours and the family never gets to see them. Who suffers? Family is so important and if you have children, you may miss their most important growing years. If you had a balancing scale, you would see that love outweighs riches and unfortunately, we may focus too much on material things. We can't take our riches with us when we die. Things must be done in moderation. This does not mean that we take away completely whatever is our defect, but we must learn to do it in moderation. We don't have to be a drunk, or a glutton, or a shop-a-holic, learn self-control and it will make our life easier. How can God bless us with more, if we don't know how to manage a little?

Another thing we have to learn to control is our feelings. We have to learn how not to have our feelings hurt so easily. An example, a person may say something to us that may seem to be offensive but they did not mean it the way we may have taken it. There have been many friendships that were destroyed because someone may have hurt someone else's feelings, intentionally or unintentionally. Remember the old saying, "sticks and stones may break my bones, but words will never hurt me." Learn not to let little things bother us and also, learn to think before we speak.

We can also stop feeling sorry for ourselves and think that we are the only one's that are suffering in this world. Sometimes, it may even feel pretty good to feel sorry for ourselves, because who else can feel sorry for us better than we can. Don't linger on self-pity, it will only bring us down. Take our problems to God and trust Him to bring us through.

With our trials, we increase in wisdom. These steps taught this couple that love, joy, peace, long-suffering, kindness, goodness, faithfulness, meekness and self-control was the best way they were able to make it through their sufferings and also these steps show us the very character of God. This is how He feels toward us, all that He wants to share with us and He is teaching us to have these qualities toward our fellow man. If we hold on to Him, if we trust Him, if we obey Him and if we patiently wait for Him, we will learn to have these same qualities each and every day of our lives and they will be a part of our character.

Our existence is a life of learning through our experiences, it can either be good or bad experiences but what we learn from them is our choice. This family has had some really rough days, some that seemed almost unbearable but God was always there, He always was.

This book's aim is not for anyone to make the same

decisions, in the same identical manner, as this family did or to make the same choices. Even if you don't agree with the choices they made or the way they chose to do things, that is all right because that is not the point of this book. The point is to take all things to God, to trust Him and always remember to thank Him; it makes no difference what choice you make or what decision you choose on how to handle your troubles, just always keep in mind that God must be our top priority and He must be first. God is a family because we are His children; He wants to take care of us, if we will let Him. Place Him in your life and bear in mind, all things will work out for good, to those who love and obey Him. Remember what Jesus Christ said, "for My yoke is easy and My burden is light." Cast all your cares on His shoulders and He will carry you through.

CHAPTER SEVEN
A Dream Come True

You glance about and observe all the heartaches, broken relationships, hatred, sickness, financial woes, and just a vision of total despair. We humans don't seem to be able to gain control of our lives or our situations. Our lives seem to be out of control. No matter where you go or whom you talk to, there is nothing but bad news. There seems to be no escapes, none at all. It is as if you are caught in someone else's life and you can't understand how you got to where you are right now. There is no more happiness and like what was discussed earlier, if you do find that happiness it is only temporary and it just slips from your fingers.

Like the famous saying on *Star Trek*, "beam me up Scotty," that is how our prayers may sound, "beam me up God." That does not mean that you don't have faith and trust in God, it only means that you are so tired of observing all that is going on around you. The ways and cares of this world just sicken you because of all the wickedness down here. You find yourself asking the questions, "whatever happened to the good old days?" But when you sit down and really think about it, were they really the good old days? Things today are getting worse and harder in order to survive, but still people had their portion of troubles. Just different times with different situations. We still had wars, people were still poor, lost jobs, sickness, hatred toward each other, famines, bad weather etc., the list could go on and on. These troubles were happening on the earth from the beginning of time.

God is such a loving Father and do you think that this was His purpose for us and that this is what He wanted for us. But look at how we have acted since man was created. Nothing to be proud of! But through it all, God still loves us and wants to give us so much. But there are things that He expects from us and right now, we are not willing to give it to Him and that is to totally surrender to Him.

That, once again, is why this family was so thankful for their trials and tribulations, because it gradually showed them how to give total surrender to God and to also permit Him to lead their life, because until God started introducing Himself to them, they were not doing such a bang up job, but since He has entered their life, they could see light at the end of the tunnel and are able to find that exit off that dark road that they so desperately are trying to find. That is what He wants for us all, to be able to get to know Him.

Did you at any time have a dream that was so exceptional and you just didn't want to wake up from that dream? Well let's right now, take ourselves into a dream, one that I'm certain you will want to continue, one that you will not want to awaken from. Okay, let's all lie down and close our eyes and relax and transfer ourselves into a deep, peaceful sleep and into a dream that will take us far, far away from this present world.

What is that extraordinary scent? It is a fragrance that seems so familiar, but there are so many distinct aromas, that it is difficult to pick one distinct scent. You glance around to attempt to see if you can detect where that wonderful scent is coming from and your eyes view a spectacular vision of the most beautiful garden that you have ever seen, one that has many special types of flowers and plants and they are all arranged and brought about in such a meticulous appearance. As you stroll along, you become aware that your feet are against this magnificent dense, green grass. It stretches as far as the eye can see. You notice, also, the various types of fruit trees, with the largest, most flawless fruit dangling from it. There are so many trees to choose from. They, too, are arranged to excellence, eager for anyone to select. There are some apples, some oranges, some grapefruits, some bananas, so many, whatever you desired, it was there. You decide to pick an apple. It was enormous. You have never seen an apple so big. You take your first bite. It was so juicy that the juice just drips down your arm and it tastes so sweet, just like pure sugar. "Where are you," you ask? You look around and you just see perfection and such elegance. Look at all the flowers. The many different colors and types and if you look closely, you could see the bees just going in and out doing their job. One thing that you notice, there are no weeds. None to be found. Everything was so manicured. You have to find out just who does the landscaping around here.

As you proceed on your walk, you notice vegetables growing. You start thinking about your first garden and how delicious your vegetables were. But these, these were special. They did not have one flaw on them. They were perfect in shape, size and color. You noticed all the leafy vegetables and not one bug hole appeared on them, everything was to perfection. Again, there were no weeds and no harmful bugs that disturbed the garden. There was so much vegetation that could feed an array of people. So many types of vegetables, some you have never seen before and some that looked familiar and some you did not know their names. With all the innumerable flowers, fruits and vegetables growing all around, the fragrances that you are smelling is so impressive that you can't even describe.

Now that you have completed using the senses of sight and smell, you now focus to the sense of hearing. You become aware of the symphony that is sounding through the air. Not by the hand made instruments of man, but of the God given instruments of birds. The many different sounds that are so cheerful and so harmonious. You sit in the middle of the field and rest and take pleasure from the various sounds of the birds. Again, some of the sounds are familiar, but some aren't. Such harmony and they all reach their pitch. They are putting on a show that is made up of numerous musicians. You open your eyes and watch them fly about. Such perfection! Their wings angled perfectly. After their flight, they would land in one of the trees and just sing their hearts out. While you are sitting and watching the show, your eye looks up to the most beautiful sky. It is so blue with such white fluffy clouds. The sun is also shining so bright. There is something different about this day. Something you can't entirely put your finger on. It doesn't make you afraid, in fact, you are enjoying this day and you don't want it to end. You decide you'd better get up and begin your stroll again because there is so much to see and you don't want to avoid a thing.

As you are walking, you hear the noise of water gushing. You are a little thirsty from all the hiking, that you take yourself over to where you hear the sound of the water. As you are moving closer, you notice the most beautiful, the most spectacular waterfall you have ever seen. The water is crystal clear, almost like glass. You follow the current of the falls and you notice that it leads into a body of water that is as blue as the sky. You look into the water and you can see straight down to the bottom. The water is so clear. You walk over and scoop some of the water into your hand to drink. It tastes so cold and fresh. It is so good! It sure beats that water you are use to drinking from the faucet. Again, you wonder to yourself, "where am I?" This place is like paradise.

You start getting a little fatigued and decide that you will get some rest now. You have done a lot of walking and investigating, so now you'll collect some food and then try to get some sleep. You think to yourself, this is definitely out of the ordinary, sleeping outdoors with the outside world and gathering your food from trees and plants, in actuality, you have never even gone camping or even took a nap outside, much less getting ready to spend the entire night outdoors but somehow you feel like everything will be all right and you are not fearful. In fact, you have a feeling of peace, like you have never felt before. You feel as though there is someone watching over you and is taking care of you and that you have absolutely nothing to fear. So you run along and gather your food. There is just so much to choose from. You always enjoyed a good salad, so off you go to your very own outdoor grocery store and you choose the finest salad that money can't buy. You gather various types of lettuce, some spinach, some celery, some radish, some cucumber, some peppers, some onions, some carrots and to top it off with the juiciest tomatoes that just squirted juice all over. You decide to conclude your meal with some fruit, maybe an orange and a banana and some figs. You almost missed some olives to put into your salad and to have some fresh, clear cold water to wash down your meal. The vegetables are so tender and fresh. Everything is just melting in your mouth. It is all so tasty. Imagine, no sprays on the foods to kill the bugs and humans, no polluted water that tastes disgusting, no dried up fruit that stayed in the stores for who knows how long and to eat in the serene ambiance of God's creation. As night started to enter, you look at the brilliance of the moon and the stars. The universe was so bright. The sky was so unclouded and you felt like you were up there sitting on top of a star. There were no city lights to clash with the expansive universe, you watched and enjoyed all that your eyes could see. You were surrounded by God. You felt so safe and you just laid your head down on the softest grass and had the finest sleep you have ever had, you slept like a baby cradled in their father's arms.

You rouse to the sounds to the singing of the birds and to one more sunny, clear day. The temperature is so perfect. It is neither too hot nor too cold, with positively no humidity in the air. This was another wonderful day, one to start out in new discoveries. But first, you go and bath in the river. This was a new experience, not washing in a sink or a shower but in a river. You felt so relaxed with the warm water from the sun hitting your skin. It gave you an extra helping hand to prepare for you journey, but after your wash up, you needed something to eat. This morning you have a taste for a nice, big, fresh, juicy melon. And was it fresh and juicy! After you finished, you noticed you had to wash up again and get the drippings from the juice off your arms. Well, now you are rested, washed, well fed and ready to go. You are off to see what else you will uncover.

As the fragrance continued to fill the air and the birds continued to sing, you happened to see unusual motion coming from somewhere within the trees. You decided to proceed a little closer and you observed something peering back at you, it was a beautiful deer. He was busy munching away on some grass and enjoying his breakfast. After he finished, he decided that he would keep you company as you continued walking along the green grass. You could not help but notice the abundance of vegetables, fruit trees and flowers. There were endless amounts. It was as though anyone could just select whatever they wanted to eat and did not have to pay because there was no one around and it looked so enticing. This was a little bizarre because who ever gave you something for nothing. But here it was, all there to feed the hungry. There was even grazing land for your new friend, whom you named Beauty. It was delightful to have some company, having a friend to talk to even though he didn't answer but he looked as though he understood what you were saying. The unusual thing was that Beauty was not afraid of you and you were not afraid of him. It was as though this deer belonged to you for many years and you both had joined together a bond of friendship. Beauty was not afraid of anything. He ran about, from one end to the other and he was at peace in this strange New World. You continued to question, "where are you?" and yet you were not afraid and also, wherever you were, you knew you did not want to leave.

As you and Beauty skipped on, you detected yourself singing to the music in the air, to the melody of the birds. You soon discovered the birds to be friendly also. On occasions, they would fly and land right next to you. Some landed on Beauty and he didn't even seem to mind. It was as though he and the birds were genuine friends. The birds even landed on your shoulder every now and then and you would all go pouncing off together. As you all went on down the grassland, you would accumulate extended friendships, some squirrels, some rabbits, some dogs, some cats, some horses, some cows and even some sheep. And guess what, each and every one of them got along. No one tried to harm the other. Even the dogs got along with the cats and the cats got along with the birds. All were together, happy and free and more importantly, at peace. This was absolutely beyond belief!

Now as you continued your expedition, you and your entourage, all were enjoying every step of the way. You started noticing the elegance of the trees. How green its leaves were and the branches stretched out with such force. You saw some beautiful maple trees growing with syrup just oozing from it. You had to go over and just taste it. It was the finest quality syrup you have ever put to your mouth. It was priceless. This was what you would call pure maple syrup. You passed by some oak trees with acorns falling from it. It was so adorable to watch the squirrels running over to collect some to eat. As many times as you have seen squirrels, you had never been so close, that the squirrels would eat immediately from your hand. All these animals were so loyal with each other and you. It was though you all were just one big happy family! There was positively no fear, none at all.

You were so thrilled of all your discoveries, you never noticed that time were speeding by and you had not eaten a thing since morning. Back to nature you went and selected some vegetables and fruit to eat and some delicious cold water to drink. You noticed that as you sat to eat your meal, that the animals also joined in the meal festivities and the entire group seemed to be enjoying their food from the ground. While you were relaxing on the blanket of green grass, digesting your meal, you happened to see some movement and it seemed to be coming toward you. You could not really make out exactly what it was but you could see the grass parting partially as this living thing proceeded to come in your direction. None of the animals seemed to pay any attention, they continued to eat. But you were nosy and wanted to know what this was. So you got up from the grass and decided to move forward, toward the direction of the movement that you were observing. As you got closer, you could see the hint of something long and so you continued to move even closer and then to your findings, you saw one of your biggest fears facing you, it was a snake. You did not stick around to even notice what type of snake it was and even if you did stick around, you no doubt would not have known the type because you never really wanted to hear anything about snakes except, that it was a snake. The type was not important. So you ran as fast as your feet could carry you, not looking back, not once. When you were about ten yards away, you stopped and then looked back to see if it was right behind you. You noticed that Beauty and the others never lifted their heads from eating. Why weren't they afraid? Then after a few minutes passed, this remarkable sensation of peacefulness came over you and you didn't seem to have anymore fear. It had completely disappeared, to the point that you made up your mind to go and look for that snake.

As you slowly moved ahead, watching your every step, you discovered again, that same movement in the grass coming toward you but this time you did not run, you kept going forward. And then, here you were; facing one of your biggest fears with nature; you were now face to face with a snake. The snake stopped moving when it saw you keeping an eye on it and then, all of a sudden, you decided to go over and stroke the snake. Its skin was somewhat cold and smooth and then, it decided to take its little head and rub gently your hand. Here you were friends with a snake! Whoever knew you would never believe this. You were so ecstatic that you couldn't wait to see what other adventure you would find so you decided to go on ahead and see what else you would discover. So here you were, with a forest of friends, Beauty at your side and the other animals encircling with a snake curled around your arm and off you all go.

As you all went merrily along, you saw monkeys swinging from the trees, frogs and rabbits hopping along together, the birds continued singing, owls hooting, and all the different wonderful sounds of God's creation. You soon noticed this exquisite house that was surrounded by a beautiful vegetable garden and fruit trees and also aromatic flowers of many distinct colors. This home was standing on an acre of land. It looked so cozy. You could smell the scent of food just coming from this house. You looked to see if there was someone moving about. You could detect, from a distance, children playing and so you decide to follow the sound. As you move closer, you could hear the children laughing, like they were having lots of fun. You saw several trees ahead and that was the same direction that the sounds were coming from. As you peered through the trees, there you saw the children running and jumping around. They seemed to be playing some game. They didn't see you, but you watched from a distance with the biggest smile on your face. They were so happy.

All of a sudden, you see this child, about three or four years old, riding on the back of some animal. You looked and just knew that your eyes were playing tricks on you. There you saw this child riding on the back of the biggest male lion you had ever seen. This had to be a big joke. This lion could not be real. There had to be a person inside of this lion's skin pretending to be a real lion. But to your wonderment, this was a real live lion, with teeth and claws and all, with a child sitting on top of his back holding on to his neck. Your first instinct was to go and run and save the child, but not far behind this lion and child came this little girl's parents. What was on their mind to allow this to happen? But then, you started to think of all the things that you have seen and witnessed yourself, thus far and all was quite remarkable and all of a sudden the fear left and the calm came. You proceeded ahead to introduce yourself to this family. As their eyes saw you, they all ran over to greet you. They were the friendliest and warmest people you have ever met. They, too, had a sense of peace and happiness, just like your little friends, the animals. They invited you into their home. As you entered inside, you immediately felt the feeling of being gladly received and belonging. The aroma of food filled the air with different scents. They asked you to eat with them and you graciously accepted. They served you baked salmon, fresh green vegetables that were steamed, potatoes, homemade wine and freshly baked apple pie. The food was delicious and you enjoyed every bite. You felt as though you had known these people forever.

You had not had such a good time in a long time. This family asked if you had a place to sleep and you said that you had been enjoying the beauty of the outdoors. They opened their home to you and invited you to stay. These people had just met you, you were a stranger to them and they invited you into their home. How could there be a place on this earth, which had people that had so much love for their fellow man. This family told you, that tomorrow they would help you find a place to live. After dinner, you helped the wife with the dishes and you both had such a wonderful conversation. You spoke about the little girl riding on the back of the lion and how brave she was. She explained that man and beast live together and that no one harms the other and that they all take care of each other. You found that thoroughly interesting because you had never heard of anything like that before.

After you both had finished the dishes, you and the family went outside to just rest after a day of chores. You all sat on the porch and you had the most relaxing sensation. There was no television, no radio, no tape player or CD's, just enjoying this awesome magnificent universe. Viewing the skies, listening to the animals and having good beneficial conversation. You all even entertained each other. You had a sing-a-long and the children danced and sang for everyone. The children even put on a show with the animals. You could not believe what you were seeing. You saw little children, from ages 3-14 years of age and these little ones were playing with some lions, tigers, bears, wolves, lambs, sheep, dogs, cats, monkeys, snakes, deer, elephants, alligators, you name it, they were there, all playing together as one, no one fighting, no one snarling, nothing but compatibility and to top it all off, these animals were playing with children. How could this be? Again you wonder, "where are you?" But you knew, wherever it was, you did not want to leave...

Did you ever feel so tranquil, that every part of your body was so at ease that you felt like you could sleep for days? But you knew you wouldn't because you could not wait for the next day. This was your first night with this family and you settled into your room and your bed for a good night's sleep. Before entering your bed, you got on your knees and prayed that God would not take you from this place, wherever it was. It was a place that you knew that man always hungered for, but did not find and you knew that you did not want to leave. After your prayer, you get into bed and view from a large open window, the vision of limitless sky, illuminated by the moon and stars, this is your soothing, as you drift off to sleep. What a dazzling view. You had the finest sleep ever. When you awoke the next morning, you felt so restored and the first thing your nostrils were able to inhale was the whiff of breakfast cooking. You leaped out of bed, washed up and eagerly skipped downstairs to be greeted by the wife. She was in the middle of cooking breakfast. Her menu consisted of fresh eggs and freshly baked bread. It, too, was mouth watering. Her husband was already outside accomplishing his chores and the children were assisting. The entire family worked together in unity and gladly helped each other without anyone telling them what their assignment was; all knew exactly what they had to do.

You had a chat with the wife that morning and told her about your first day in this unfamiliar place and how you had discovered all the vegetables and fruit trees growing for anyone to choose from. You questioned if that was acceptable because you had taken a few to eat on your journey and should you make restitution. She explained that it is grown especially for the needy to select from and to eat as they are on their journey and that it is unconditionally free. " Free," you thought to yourself? "Who gives you anything for free?" This was too good to believe. You questioned to yourself, if this was the planet earth? Where are you? But again, wherever it was, you wanted to stay.

After breakfast, you helped tidy up and also with some of the chores. This family was so generous, so tender and affectionate, they wanted to make sure you were all right. You went outside and found the ground was wet. You asked the wife if it had rained last night. She answered that it did and that whenever it does rains it does so at night. I questioned if they had any problems with drought or famine and she answered that they did not. She explained that it rains only when it is necessary and also the food grows in abundance and it feeds everyone. She explained that they had neither drought nor famine in all the earth. That all of God's creatures and human beings ate; there was no starvation in the entire world. With her saying that, you had to sit down and allow all that she was telling you sink in. You believed it because of all that you had seen. But to be in such a place that all ate and that there was absolutely no starvation, it actually brought tears of joy to your eyes.

The day was radiant. As this family did their chores, you lent a helpful hand whenever and wherever you were needed.

The wife needed to go into town to buy some items and she asked if you wanted to go. So the two of you left the others and walked to town, it was not too far away from where they lived. As you were walking, you observed how everything was so clean. You passed by homes and each had an acre of land. Not only was everything so clean, the gardens were so manicured with no weeds and no stray leaves and grew in nice rich soil. Everything was so abundant. The neighbors that were outside working, waved as you passed by. Some came over to you both and you were introduced. Everyone was so friendly and so caring and more importantly, so loving. You met some people of different colors and different nationalities and each and everyone seemed to get along and treat each other with love and respect.

This family you just met asked if you had a home to live in. You told them no and that you were new in town. They told you that they had a home that they could let you live in, if you liked it. You told them that you really did not have much money to pay for it because you did not have a job as of yet. They said that it was all right, that they had this home ready for someone who was a stranger and needed somewhere to live. So they took you down to where the house was. It was such a lovely house and you were quite satisfied. You asked yourself, how could these people be so kind to you, they did not even know you. You felt so at ease with them all, like you had been friends forever. So, of course, you said yes, that you would be honored to stay in their guesthouse. You knew that you had to hurry and get a job, not that you felt pressured, but you wanted to start paying rent and not take advantage.

So you and the wife continued your walk to town and you thought that you could try and get a job there. As you approached town, the people, also, were very sociable. Everyone said hello and asked how were things going and they really were concerned about their neighbor. We went into a textile store so the wife could buy some material. You inquired about being hired for a job. You were introduced to the owner of the store. Everyone seemed to know everyone. The owner and his wife were also very cordial. They said that they could use some assistance and employed you right on the spot. You loved the job, not only were the owners a devoted couple, so was everyone who entered the store. The store owners never locked any doors to the shops. There were no alarms, no security devices anywhere. Everyone trusted each other. In fact, there was absolutely no crime at all in the entire town. How could this be? No crime at all!!!!!

You thought to yourself, this must be only in this one town. One day, you picked up a newspaper and you started noticing that the paper was filled only of good things, not one morsel of crime spoken of. You inquired from the owner; didn't this paper report any crimes throughout the world? The owner told you that every person on the face of the earth obeyed all the laws that were brought into existence and there was not one bit of crime. There were no wars, no murder, and no stealing, not even any laws broken against their neighbor. This world was an environment of peace and love. Now you thought to yourself, you must have hit your head. Who was this lawgiver, one that enforced these laws and that everyone obeyed? Who could this be? You knew that man kept promising peace each and every year with no success, but who was this lawgiver who finally found the way to peace. You could not wait to meet him.

When you got your first paycheck, you went to pay your rent to the family who owned the property where you were staying. They told you, that they did not want you to pay them rent, but wanted you to save your money to be able to buy your very own home. You could not believe the words that you were hearing. Pay no rent! The people that you met in this town were so considerate, with feeding you, giving you shelter and also giving you clothing to wear until you were able to save enough money to buy your own home.

That time came quickly. You had sufficient funds to now seek for your new home. You found this beautiful home and it had such a cozy feeling. It, too, was like all of your surroundings, it had a feeling of peace and serenity. It was a home that you could live in forever. The landscaping was so impressive. You had a small stream a short distance from your house. It had an abundance of fish swimming about. You could go to sleep to the sound of the water rippling and the night sounds.

Another thing, have you ever heard of such a place where everyone was commanded by this lawgiver to have twenty-four hours of rest, every man and every beast? Who was this lawgiver? You could not wait to be introduced to him. The way you found out about this day of rest was while at work. You heard people speaking about going home early so that they could prepare their meals and to get things ready and in order, to anticipate twenty-four hours of rest and fellowship. In the beginning of this day of rest, you were invited to one of your new friend's home. They had invited you to dinner and to meet some neighbors. You could not wait. You decided to bake a peach pie from your peach tree, in your very own yard and you would bring it their home. It was almost time to leave, so you grabbed your pie that looked and smelled so delicious and you started down the road to their home. You were there promptly at 6:00PM. That was the time they told to come and as you entered their home, four other guests greeted you. One was a pleasant gentleman that seemed to be interested in you. You engaged in some really wholesome conversation and he, like everyone else, was so warm and kind. You felt quite comfortable talking to him. He invited you to go with him, in the morning, to the city, where all meet to go to worship the Creator of all, the lawgiver. You were so ecstatic because you were going to meet this lawgiver, the one who was able to bring peace and happiness to all that obeyed his laws. So you accepted, gracefully. After dinner, you all went to go and sit on the front porch. Like each night, this too was a very serene night. You all continued to talk and just relax. How could there be a day, a full day, when everyone just rested and gazed at all of God's creation. You noticed the animals that helped with the farming chores, they too, were resting. It was true, every man and beast obeyed this law, happily.

The next day was finally here and you were so excited, not only to be able to be with your new gentleman friend, but to go to the city and to worship God and be able to meet this lawgiver. Your gentleman friend came and picked you up; right on time and you both traveled to the city. When you arrived, you could not believe it. It was beautiful, it was spectacular. The streets were so clean. There were no tall buildings were people lived or worked on top of each other. People walking about laughing and playing as they went along. There was the old with the young, all having a good time. They were all going to this place, this building to worship their God on this special day, this weekly day that He commanded all to obey. When you entered the building, you saw its elegance inside and outside. It was the greatest service you had ever been too. These people were all of one accord. There were no people of different beliefs, or different religions. They were of one mind. This was throughout the entire earth. There were no confusions. All spoke the same thing... This was a place that taught all of God's laws and how much God loved us and what He wanted to give us, if we obey Him. These people hungered to please their God. You finally met this Lawgiver; it was God, Himself. This was astounding; everything just started falling into place. We all have finally accepted what God wanted to give us all along but were too self-seeking to accept it. Since the day that you first stepped your foot in this remarkable area, this was the best day of all. You have accepted all that God was teaching you and wanted to continue learning His teachings and you wanted their God to be your God. You, too, wanted to obey God. You were a part of this place and yes, you wanted to stay, more now than ever before. As you were leaving this building, you looked around and saw a sign that read "Welcome To My World." Tears just ran down your face, you saw that we all had a God that wanted every living creature of this earth to be happy, truly happy. A happiness that would last forever! You could not wait until next week to be here with many different people from all types of backgrounds, races, nationalities, you name it, and all were now together as one.

Time passed and you and your gentleman friend got married. You and he lived in the beautiful home that you purchased. You were now a family in this New World, where you knew that you belonged. As time went on, you became pregnant several times. Several is the operative word, you had seven children. God had issued a promise, that all would be fruitful and multiply and as you can see, that promise, like all the others, were kept. Not only for you, but also for all. There was not one barren woman throughout all the land. Could you imagine that, not one? You and your husband brought your children up in the teachings of God's laws.

Being a wife and mother is a very fulfilling part of your life. Your day would begin with you awakening early in the morning before your family arises. The house is nice and quiet, so you begin to start your day before sunrise. Your husband is an early riser also, because he is a farmer and you want him to begin his day with a healthy breakfast. You open your day by fixing your morning meal. You first start by making some freshly baked bread and while that is baking, you would go and gather some fresh fruit and also some eggs. So while you would be preparing the meal, your husband would awaken to the smells of bread baking. After he would wash up and dress, he'd come downstairs to his cooked breakfast. You would sit and eat with him and both of you would share what your plans were for the day. Then you would kiss him and off to work he'd go. You would even prepare enough food for the workers to munch on while they did their job. After you would care for the workers, you would prepare the children for school and provide them with a well-balanced meal and send them on their way. While they are gone, you would finish the chores around the house and decide what you would do for the day. You noticed that the children needed some clothes because they were outgrowing theirs, so you went to the fabric store to buy some material to make them some clothes. You happen to see some nice material that you would buy, so you decided to make your husband a nice pair of pants. You always chose the finest in material because you wanted your family dressed in quality. You also bought some material to make some clothing to sell. You worked from your home because you wanted to raise your children and care for your husband. When you were finished, you went home and would put aside the clothing that was too small for your children and give them to those that had less.

You noticed that your husband's business was expanding in farming and that he needed additional land. You went to investigate several fields to see what was best for your husband's needs and also, what would be a good location so that he could grow food for people that may be hungry and that they would be able to pick on their way. You remembered how you were fed when you first came to this place and you always wanted to follow the example of giving and so you did. You located the exact section of land that you were looking for and you purchased it. Your husband trusted you in these types of decisions, you were his helpmate. You knew that he was too busy to stop his work and take time to look for property, so you helped by taking care of this part of the business for him. Real estate was in your hands.

Through the seasonal changes in the weather, your family does not have to fret because you take care of them with garments that can deal with whatever the temperature may be. With the clothing that you make you also sell to help with the expenses of your household. Your husband is so pleased with you and how you take care of them all. He always seems to be singing your praises. He loves you so much and so do your children. They all know that they can rely on you always and that your commitment is faithful. Your husband says that your value is more than all the riches of the world.

You are a competent individual. One that puts her trust in God and doesn't allow problems to distress her. People come to you for helpful hints because you speak words of wisdom. Your children are growing up to be strong, trustworthy, respectful human beings, one's that you are pleased with. Your example is an example that others follow, because you are kind and generous to others. You know how an individual can be the most beautiful person on the outside but are ugly on the inside because they may have a really bad disposition? But to have that inner beauty, that is what appeals to the eyes of others. What you do in your life that is how people will remember you.

This is a woman that has much love for God, for her family and her neighbor. Is there such a woman? This woman works diligently to keep her family mended together, with her husband who is the one in charge of his family and she is his helpmate and they both work jointly to bring together a happy family. This is what we all want to strive to be, one that is strong but not overpowering, loving but not smothering, a worker but not a fanatic. We are to have our priorities in place. That is our goal, not to lead but be led by the one, true leader of all, God Almighty.

Another wonderful blessing that our God has given to His children and that is, there is no more sickness. There was not one hospital on all the earth. Can you believe it, no sickness? All mankind finally recognized what God was trying to pump into our heads all the time and that was that He and He alone is, and always was our Healer. When or if anyone got sick with anything, they would simply go to their Healer, inform Him, trust Him and have faith in Him that He would take care of the illness. With obedience and faith, guess what, God did what He promised and He would heal them. The lame walked, the deaf could hear, the blind was able to see, all diseases were taken from off the face of the earth. Everyone lived a life free from disease. There was no one walking around with someone else's body parts in their body, of missing body parts because someone removed a body part from you, nor was anyone all cut up like a piece of beef from an operation. No one experimented on animals or humans trying to find answers because God had revealed all the answers. No one walked around all doped up or with all kinds of side effects from the many different medications that they were given while trying to get better. You didn't have every kind or type of foreign object stuck into every part of your body to be tested while trying to see what was wrong. No more telethons to raise money for research to find cures for some incurable disease. There were no false promises of healing because only God heals. You see, our Lawgiver gave us laws on how to keep ourselves free from sickness and guess what, all obeyed those laws and He kept His promises. It was such a wonderful thing to see, everyone feeling great, each and everyday. The young and the old, all were free from pain and sickness.

The next thing that you saw, was how the government was organized. There was no such thing that each country, state, town etc. would have their own government structure. The entire earth consisted of only one government. They had a king that was in charge of all the earth, then there were twelve in charge of different areas, then there were priests and judges that made sure each nation kept the laws that were established, you also had rulers of each city that would uphold the law that came from the one in charge and then you had the teachers, they were the ones that taught God's laws to mankind. Last but not least, the One that was in charge of all, the Head, the Lawgiver was Jesus Christ, who is the King of kings and the Lord of lords. He was the One that made these laws and distributed a government to make sure that all His laws were being kept. There was absolutely no voting in politicians, no man-made government that would promise you things that they could and would not keep. This government was made of people that were put in by God, Himself. This government kept their promises that were made and was interested in the people and not themselves and what they could get. Each and every person knew what their job consisted of; they did it well and in harmony. Now is that a government or not? One that you could be pleased to be a part of. There was no corruption, no backbiting, and no one stepping on the other to get to the top and no lies!!!! This government was a government that was for the people. This is one that we all will love and that is no jury duty! There were no court cases because there were no crimes. So, of course, that meant there were no lawyers. There were no lawsuits because all followed the laws that were placed by the government on how to treat one another, so that meant that no one would take his neighbor to court to sue another; each person was taught how to handle any situation, they did no intentional damage to the other and if there was any accidental damage done, it was handled in a giving and loving way and that was put into force by the Lawgiver. This was a government of giving and not getting and that taught all mankind to love each other no matter what, to live at peace with one another and to love our God with our whole mind, heart and soul. Could it get any better? This was a government that all appreciated and respected, one that all hungered and thirsted to obey. This was a government that if its people obeyed, blessings would come from their obedience, not only individually but also worldwide.

As you enrolled your first child in school, you were so pleased with their educational system. These teachers were taught how to train these children in the way to have a purposeful and successful life in all aspects. They are taught all the fundamentals, reading, writing and arithmetic. The most prominent thing that stood out and was so astonishing was that each and every person on the face of the earth spoke one language. It was a language that God formed, so that each and every person could communicate with one another. It was a language that pleased Him. It gave you a sense of oneness with people who may live all the way on the other side of the globe. You could travel anywhere in the world and not feel like a stranger because all could understand each other. The teachers also gave the children a good foundation, which started with who God is and consisted of His laws, which are His Ten Commandments. They taught these little ones how much their Father loved them and all He does and will do for them.

They are shown how they can love their God and please Him and how they can love their neighbors and do good to them. They are also shown how to obey their parents and honor them. They are shown how to bring and continue to have peace on the earth. They are taught to respect and love themselves and others and how to pray for one another. They are molded into being individuals that will become a well-rounded adult and that are taught the one basic word... LOVE. They were also taught how to trust their God and that they could go to Him for anything. Their parents also followed up all that was taught to the children in school, at home, not only by words but also by their example. So this also helped with maintaining a strong, loving family life. They were also taught other subjects that would provide them with skills in obtaining a job one-day and helping them reveal what they wanted to be. Everything went hand in hand; God always came first and then themselves. They knew that it was God that was leading their little lives and whatever they wanted to be, they would go and pray and allow God to lead them; they knew that He must come first in order to have proper success. This was the greatest education that you could have ever seen or heard about and it was absolutely free. There were no drop outs and all excelled with high grades. No one was made to feel inferior and whatever weakness they may have, there were people there to assist them. There was no competition with one another; everyone went at their own pace and comfort. No one got left back because all succeeded and all excelled into being very respectful, successful individuals, living the way of God.

Yes, welcome to God's world. It is a world full of peace, joy and love. Does all this seem too good to be true? Does this seem like it is too far fetched, one that will never happen? Are we all on this planet now, awaiting something better or are we just existing and going through this life with no purpose and no future and then the finale, which is, death? Whatever you think, one thing we all would agree, wouldn't it be wonderful if this world of dreams could or will be called the world of today..

She awakens to the sound of the alarm. She rubs her eyes trying to see where she is. She recognizes that she is in the same place she was in when she went to sleep that night. She sits on the side of the bed, a little confused. She looks at the clock and sees it is 6:30, she looks outside and sees the sun out and hears the birds singing, so she says to herself, "it must be morning." She feels as though she had been asleep for days. She feels so rested and so at peace within herself. She thought about all that was rolling around in her head and wondered to herself, "was it a dream or was it for real?" "It must have been a dream," she thought. But it felt so real. She looks around and saw her husband in the bed next to her, he was still sleeping.

As she continued sitting on the edge of the bed, somewhat dazed, her life started resurfacing, she was now remembering all that she and her husband had gone through and that her troubles were still there. She then realized that while she was asleep, that she was having a wonderful dream and that her real life was a nightmare. She started asking God to wake her up from this nightmare and to help her to go back to her dream and to make that her real life. As she sat, she became a little depressed. She started reminiscing about their little girl and wondered where she could be and how she is, she remembered her husband was blind and out of work, she remembered their financial woes and how they could barely make ends meet and last but not least, she remembered they never had their baby from their own body. And then, she had this feeling of emptiness that entered her body and she felt so all alone and so helpless. She now had tears streaming down her face. What was now happening, the fantasy was disappearing and the reality was now appearing. But then she started thinking, was her dream true or just that, a dream? But no matter what it was, fact or a fiction, it still meant the same thing and that is, if we do what God wants us to do, just like the dream, God's promises were still the same, past, present and future. You still have a God that is with you and He promises that He will never leave you or forsake you and if we do what He says, He will deliver you.

She started feeling much better and got up to start housekeeping. She told her husband about her dream and it encouraged them to realize how they will continue to have God in their life and let Him lead them in the direction He wanted them to go. They would continue to trust Him and have faith in Him. They would continue to have patience and know that He will deliver them when and how He wants to. They knew that God wanted to give mankind a better way of life, but we had to exercise responsibility and wait patiently. We must love our God, with our entire mind, heart and soul and know that He loves us. We can all one day have a dream and in our dream we can see a sign that will read, "Welcome to God's World" and maybe it won't be a dream, it may be our brand new world.

I know that this couple had been through an assortment of troubles. It looks like a life of hopelessness, but I can guarantee that they do not have a life of hopelessness. Yes, what was said formerly, life got and still gets very painful and heart wrenching, but they continue to move onward and trust in their God. There are reasons that I have so much information relating to this couple and also can be so outspoken with you, is because my husband and I are that couple. So everything that is written is coming to you firsthand. We have been through many trials and tribulations, but what had been said in a previous chapter, when the going gets tough, the tough get going. Like I also voiced earlier, my husband and I did not create this book so that people would proceed to handle situations in the manner in which we did or to completely agree with the way we chose to deal with our difficulties, but only to know that whatever troubles you are having, no matter what, don't be frightened or embarrassed, because you can go to God for anything. You can talk to Him and you can cry with Him, everything remains private between you and Him. By no means does any person have to know a thing that you may not want to share with anybody. You don't have to be apprehensive, all you have to do is communicate with Him and you will find out that He is not judgmental. He is compassionate and continuously eager to listen. He tells us to ask Him anything, seek for an answer and then knock and He will open the door and invite you in. Try it, it may help.

We wanted to acquaint you to our Majestic and Wonderful God. One that is above all and knows all. We did not want you to contemplate going to God simply when you are in trouble and you need His immediate help and that you only need Him in your life just for that instant. That is why we are to be developing by the unpredictable changes of our lives, so that we can grow to have a relationship with our God, each and every day and every waking minute of our lives, because we need Him, not just when we are in trouble but always and forever. That is the single most important way that we can learn to know Him and He us. Do not purely have a relationship with God only to get because that is not the relationship that He wants for us. God's focus is only on giving. Yes, we have had various adversities in our twenty-nine years of marriage and I am confident we will go through more because that is how we mature. All through the many years, we received many gifts that God had faithfully bestowed to us. Yes, everyday we awaited for the gifts of our heart's desire, which were the loss of my husband's vision, our financial problems, the baby from our body and for our daughter to return home. Those gifts we so desperately desired, but the greatest gift of all was right in front of us all along. That gift from God was not something that was physical, which can be taken away from us. That gift from God was God, Himself. He gave my husband and I an opportunity to become acquainted with Him and get to know Him each day of our lives and to dwell with Him forevermore. What an awesome gift, one that can never be substituted. One that you will never exchange for anything else. This gift, I am sure, you will want to keep. We both will revere and respect our gift throughout eternity.

Well, it appears that we have come to the completion of our adventure and it was fun for us to travel with you and finding new discoveries along the way. Our road may have been rugged with lots of twists and turns but, through it all, we prevailed and we have experienced plenty. We will try to put forth an effort to no longer take for granted all that God has created and we will strive to esteem it entirely, from the smallest to the greatest. The point of this book is to divulge that you have a God that loves you and wants to acquaint Himself to you, it is not based on, if and how God delivered this family from our trials. We positively did not want anyone to believe that the only important thing in life is to be free from whatever our difficulty. We learn from our distresses, treasure that. But I will tell you this, that the Princess and her Prince Charming lived happily ever after. Remember, the motto of this book is, "All things work together for good, to those who love God."

My husband and I truly hope that you found pleasure from reading this book and that it will be instrumental with you getting to know our Father. We hope that it will reveal to you that the fantasy we may have, can become a reality. But we have to, foremost, read God's educational book that He wrote for us and understand His desire for His children and perhaps with us abiding by His words, we, too, will be privileged to locate that light that shines so bright at the end of the tunnel and so that you can take possession of your marvelous gift from God. This book is a love story between God and us. We find out how to have an intimate relationship with Him. We can make this love affair endure or fail; the choice is ours. If our decision is to please Him, we are sure He will never leave us nor forsake us.

Printed in the United Kingdom
by Lightning Source UK Ltd.
9714700001B/20